Archives in Appalachia: A Directory

Ellen Garrison
Editor

The Appalachian Consortium was a non-profit educational organization composed of institutions and agencies located in Southern Appalachia. From 1973 to 2004, its members published pioneering works in Appalachian studies documenting the history and cultural heritage of the region. The Appalachian Consortium Press was the first publisher devoted solely to the region and many of the works it published remain seminal in the field to this day.

With funding from the Andrew W. Mellon Foundation and the National Endowment for the Humanities through the Humanities Open Book Program, Appalachian State University has published new paperback and open access digital editions of works from the Appalachian Consortium Press.

www.collections.library.appstate.edu/appconsortiumbooks

ISBN (pbk.: alk. Paper): 978-1-4696-4240-6
ISBN (ebook): 978-1-4696-4241-3

Distributed by the University of North Carolina Press
www.uncpress.org

TABLE OF CONTENTS

THE APPALACHIAN CONSORTIUM

The Appalachian Consortium is a non-profit, educational organization dedicated to perserving the cultural heritage of Southern Appalachia. The organization's goals are to assist in solving current problems, to improve the quality of present and future life in the area and raise the pride of the Appalachian people in their traditions and the region in which they live. For further information, please contact the Appalachian Consortium at University Hall, Boone, NC 28608. The telephone number is 704/262-2069.

The member institutions of the Appalachian Consortium are:

Appalachian State University
Blue Ridge Parkway
East Tennessee State University
First Tennessee-Virginia Development District
Lees-McRae
Mars Hill College
North Carolina Division of Archives and History
Southern Highland Handicraft Guild
U. S. Forest Service
Warren Wilson College
Western Carolina University
Western North Carolina Historical Association

ACKNOWLEDGEMENTS

No project of this size is ever completed without help from a variety of sources, and we are grateful to all who made this directory possible. First and foremost, we thank the National Historical Publications and Records Commission for the funding which provided staff and support to mail over 1,000 questionnaires and compile the responses. We are especially grateful to Nancy Sahli and Sandra Anderson of the commission staff who answered numerous questions about the whys, wherefores, and how-tos of the project.

This directory would not exist had hundreds of librarians, archivists and curators not taken time from their already busy schedules to complete our questionnaire. A very special thanks to all of you—especially those who, owing to the vagaries of the US Postal Service, received the questionnaire only days before the deadline for return. We hope this research resource we are placing in your hands will be some compensation for your diligence in responding to our queries.

The project was planned and directed by an advisory committee consisting of at least one representative from each state included in the directory. These individuals assembled mailing lists, revised and critiqued our survey instrument, encouraged professional colleagues in each state to respond to our queries and personally followed up with potential contributors to insure that our directory would be as complete as possible. For their thoughtful and timely guidance, we wish to thank Lisle Brown, Marshall University, West Virginia; Anne Campbell, University of Kentucky; Richard Dillingham, Mars Hill College, North Carolina; Hellen Kimsey, Mountain Regional Library, Georgia; Michael Kohl, Clemson University, South Carolina; Jim Lloyd, Western Carolina University, North Carolina; Dorothy McCombs, Virginia Polytechnic Institutes and State University; and Charles Robb, Berea College, Kentucky.

Kathryn Wheelock, project coordinator, was responsible for compiling our master mailing list, producing and mailing all questionnaires, designing our directory format and inputting all data, and contacting all non-respondents by phone and in person. It is to Kathryn we owe our exceptional response rate.

Lewis Cox, a student at East Tennessee State University, assisted Ms. Wheelock in designing the computer-based format for the directory and completed work on the final phases of data entry, proof-reading, and printing after Ms. Wheelock's resignation in early 1985. To Lewis, and his mastery of our sometimes uncooperative Apple II, we owe our success in using the modern technology which baffled others on the project staff. We are also grateful to Susan Twaddle and Milt Tober of ETSU's office of computer services for their assistance in this and other phases of the project.

The leaders of the Appalachian Consortium, including Emmett Essin, chairman of the board of directors; Barry Buxton, executive director; Malinda Crutchfield, associate director; and Lois Forrester, administrative secretary, contributed not only practical help in administration and organization but much-needed moral support and encouragement. Jacqueline Stewart, assistant director of the Consortium Press, designed the directory cover and served as our advisor in production and printing of the directory. Members of the Consortium's Heritage and Folklife Committee generously gave of their time during our 1984-85 meetings to critique our survey instrument, suggest additions to our mailing list and cheer our progress.

Many individuals at East Tennessee State University supplied the expertise required to implement the project. To Abbott Brayton, director of contracts and grants; Betty Tester and Lynn Myers, comptroller's office; and Rosemary Barson, University Press, many thanks for your patience and cooperation.

Finally, we are grateful to Dr. Fred Borchuck, director of the Sherrod Library, East Tennessee State University, whose support made possible our work on this project; to the many friends in the library's division of reader services who helped compile our mailing list and answered numerous questions quickly and cheerfully; and to the loyal and devoted staff of the Archives of Appalachia, especially Kathryn Wilson and Barbara Minor, who assumed extra duties so that we might devote our time to this project.

To all of these colleagues on our own campus and elsewhere whose support, encouragement and hard work made this directory possible, thank you. For the errors and omissions which exist in spite of your best efforts, we take full responsibility.

Ellen Garrison
Archives of Appalachia
East Tennessee State University

HOW TO USE THIS DIRECTORY

This directory consists of entries describing 181 repositories in 195 counties* in south central Appalachia which hold historical records documenting the political, social, cultural, and economic history of the region, and a list of "Coming Attractions," agencies which do not currently collect manuscript materials but which plan to do so in the future. Also included are indexes by type of material and by subject which will enable researchers to locate selected genres of documentary material (e.g. photographs) or materials related to a particular subject.

The questionnaires from which this directory was compiled were mailed to all colleges and universities, public libraries, museums, historic sites, and historical and genealogical societies in the region listed in published directories and to selected secondary schools, businesses, and churches known to hold historical records. We included cultural facilities operated by federal, state, or local governments and public libraries which serve as a repository for local government records. However, we omitted facilities which operate solely as government records repositories and the two state archives (West Virginia Department of Archives and History and the Western Office of the North Carolina Division of Archives and History) in the region.

Each main entry, based on the questionnaire completed by the repository staff, includes information on the name, location, and hours of the repository; the type of respoitory; the types of material held by the repository; the broad subject areas covered by these records; the geographical area that the records cover; and the inclusive dates and size of the holdings**. We have also included the name of the staff member primarily responsible for manuscripts in each repository. Researchers are urged to contact these individuals for additional information about a repository's holdings.

The main entries are arranged first by state and second alphabetically by the name of the repository. The form of entry used for a repository depended primarily on the form used by the individual completing the questionnaire. Generally, a repository which is a division or department within a larger agency is filed and alphabetized under the name of the department or division (i.e. Special Collections) not the name of the larger agency (i.e. Berea College). However, collections of local historical or genealogical societies which are housed in public libraries are frequently listed only under the name of the public library. Also, the directory was alphabetized by a computer, and computers are intractable little beasts. Therefore all repository names are alphabetized absolutely by the first word in the name (i.e. Frank H. McClung Museum is found under "F").

Because of inconsistencies in form of entry and computer alphabetizing by perhaps unexpected first words in an entry, it is advisable to check under possible variations of a repository

* Information on the counties can be found following this section.

** Abbreviations are used for type of repository, type of material, and subjects; a key to these abbreviations precedes the "Main Entries."

name when a listing for a specific repository cannot be located. To facilitate such searches, there is a list of all repositories in each state included following the "Coming Attractions."

Each entry is numbered in the order in which it is filed, and all index citations are by this repository number. However, because duplications were discovered during final proof-reading, five entries had to be deleted after all entries were numbered. Thanks again to our intractable computer, renumbering was impossible in the time available, and therefore there are no entries for numbers 29, 105, 107, 109 and 120.

We hope this directory will provide researchers who seek to explore Appalachia's rich heritage with access to the local documentary resources which make such work possible. However, we could not include the many repositories outside the region which hold significant documentary material related to Appalachia. For information on these collections, researchers should consult the National Historical Publications and Records Commission's DIRECTORY OF ARCHIVES AND MANUSCRIPT REPOSITORIES and the NATIONAL UNION CATALOG OF MANUSCRIPTS published by the Library of Congress.

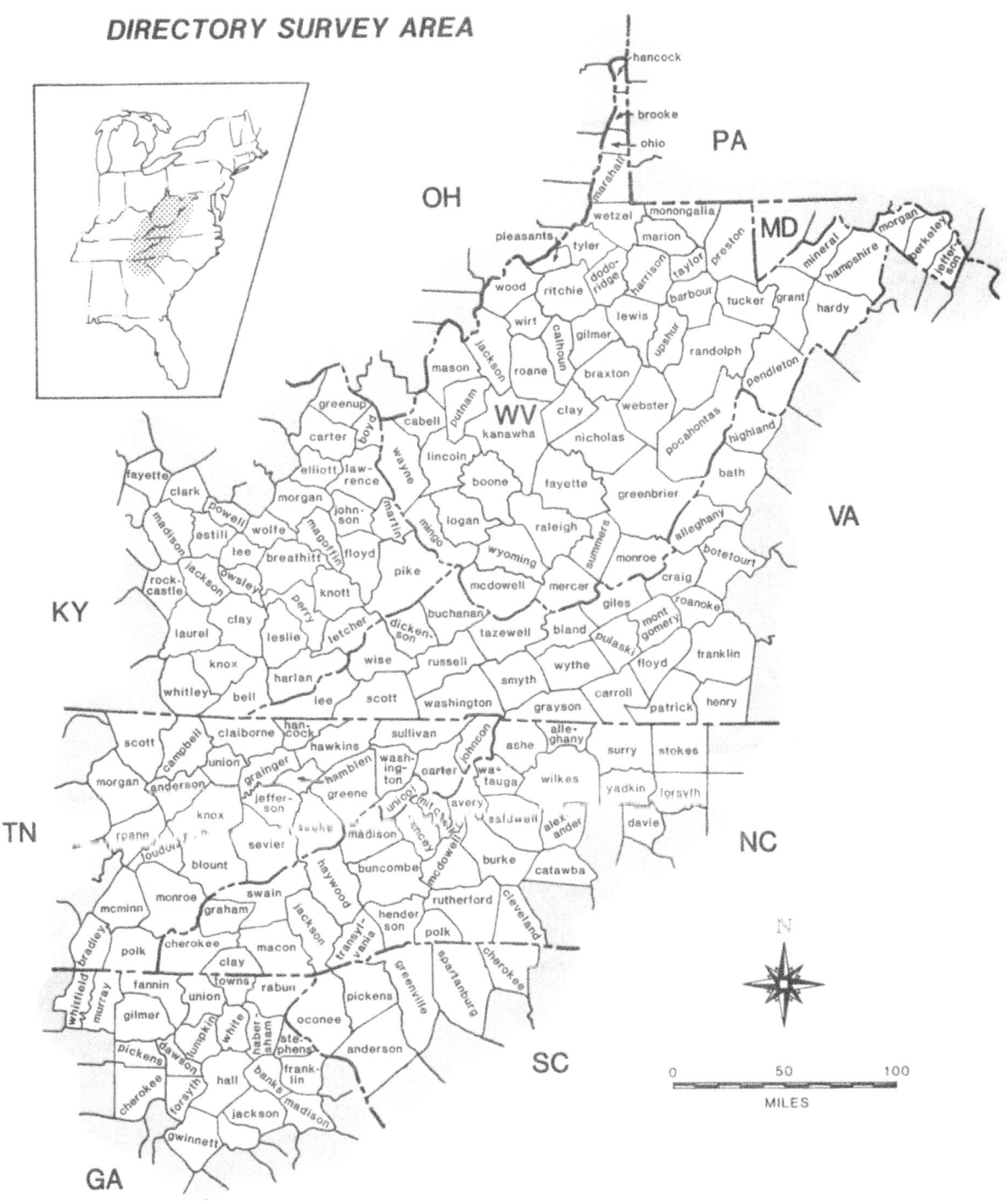

DIRECTORY SURVEY AREA

cartography by arex/rer

LIST OF ABBREVIATIONS

Repository Type

BU— Business
CS— Church/Synagogue
CU— College/University
GE— Genealogical Society
HS— Historical Society
MU— Museum
OT— Other
PL— Public Library
SS— Secondary School

Records

MS— Manuscripts
OH— Oral histories
GE— Genealogical charts
AV— Audio-video
PH— Photographs
IA— Records of parent institution

Subjects

A G — Agriculture/farming
A R — Art/architecture
B L — Blacks
B I — Business/industry
C W - Civil War
C R — Crafts
E D — Education
E I — Ethnic groups/immigration
F C — Family/community life
G E — Genealogy
H S — Health sciences
I N — Indians
L A — Labor
L I — Literature
L H — Local history
M C — Mass Communications
M H — Military History (except Civil War)
M I — Mining
M U — Music
N R — Natural resources/conservation
P A — Performing Arts (except music)
P W — Pioneers/westward expansion

P S — Politics/government: state and local
P N — Politics/government: national
R T — Recreation/tourism
R C — Religion/church history
S A — Social action
S T — Science/technology
T T — Transportation/travel
W O — Women

MAIN ENTRIES

Georgia

1 **Chattahoochee National Forest**   Records: MS, PH, IA
  U. S. Forest Service
  P. O. Box 216   Subjects: AG, CR, ED, FC, IN, MI,
  Blairsville, GA 30512   NR, PW, RT, ST

  404-745-6928   Type: OT   Geographical Area: Appalachia
  Frances Mason, Forester   Dates: 1801 to 1860, 1901 to date
  By Appointment Only   Size: 1-10 linear feet

2 **Chattahoochee-Oconee N. Forest**   Records: MS, OH, AV, PH, IA
  U. S. Forest Service
  601 Broad St.   Subjects: AG, BI, CW, CR, FC, IN, LI,
  Gainesville, GA 30501   LH, MI, NR, RT, TT

  404-536-0541   Type:OT   Geographical Area: Appalachia
  Rachel G. Schneider, Public Affairs   Dates: 1901 to date
  Mon.-Fri. 8-4:30   Size: 1-10 linear feet

3 **Crown Garden and Archives**   Records: MS, OH, GE, PH, IA
  Whitfield-Murray Historical Society
  715 Chattanooga Ave.   Subjects: CW, FC, GE, IN, LI, LH, RC
  Dalton, GA 30720

  404-278-0217   Type: HS   Geographical Area: Appalachia
  Polly Boggess, Director   Dates: 1801 to date
  Tues.-Sat. 9-5   Size: 11-50 linear feet

4 **Forsyth County Heritage Found.**   Records: MS, PH
  P. O. Box 762
  Room 040 Courthouse   Subjects: GE, IN, LH, MH, PW, RC
  Cumming, GA 30130

  404-887-1626   Type: HS   Geographical Area: Appalachia
  Don L. Shadburn, Director   Dates: Pre-1800 to date
  By Appointment Only   Size: 11-50 linear feet

5 **Fox Fire Fund, Inc.**   Records: MS, OH, AV, PH, IA
  P. O. Box B
  Rabun Gap, GA 30568   Subjects: AG, AR, BL, BI, CW, CR,
                                                   ED, EI, FC, GE, HS, LA, LH, MI,
                                                   MU, PS, PN, RT, RC, SA, ST, TT,
                                                   WO

  404-746-5318   Type: OT   Geographical Area: Appalachia
  B. Eliot Wigginton   Dates: 1801 to date
  By Appointment Only   Size: Over 1000 linear feet

6 **Gwinnett Historical Society**   Records: MS, GE, PH
P. O. Box 261
Lawrenceville, GA 30246   Subjects: FC, GE, IN, LH, PW, PS, RC

404-962-1450   Type: HS   Geographical Area: Appalachia
Jon McDaniel, Treasurer   Dates: 1801 to date
Mon.-Fri. 9-12   Size: 11-50 linear feet

7 **Marble Valley Hist. Society**   Records: MS, GE, PH
GA. Room of Pickens Co. Lib.
P. O. Box 567   Subjects: BI, CW, FC, GE, IN, LH, MI,
Jasper, GA 30143   RC

                             Type: HS   Geographical Area: Appalachia
Robert S. Davis, Jr., President   Dates: 1801 to date
Mon., Tues., Thurs., Fri. 8:30-5; Sat. 9-12 Size: 11-50 linear feet

8 **Mountain Regional Library**   Records: MS
P. O. Box 157
East Main St.   Subjects: AG, CR, FC, IN, LI, LH, PS,
Young Harris, GA 30582   RC

404-379-3732   Type: PL   Geographical Area: Appalachia
Hellen H. Kimsey   Dates: 1866 to date
8:30-5 Weekdays; 1-5 Sat.   Size: 11-50 linear feet

9 **N.E. Georgia Regional Library**   Records: GE
Jefferson and Green St.
Clarkesville, GA 30523   Subjects: GE

404-754-4413   Type PL   Geographical Area: Appalachia
Emily Anthony, Director   Dates: 1801 to date
Mon. 9-8; Tues.-Fri. 9-5; Sat. 9-1   Size: 11-50 linear feet

10 **Quinlan Art Center**   Records: MS, IA
Gainesville Art Association
514 Green St., N.E.   Subjects: AR
Gainesville, GA 30501

404-536-2575   Type: MU   Geographical Area: Appalachia
Barbara Swerens, Director   Dates: 1901 to date
Mon.-Fri. 10-4   Size: 1-10 linear feet

11 **Sequoyah Regional Library**   Records: MS, OH, PH
400 East Main St.   Subjects: BI, CW, ED, GE, IN, LA, LI,
Canton, GA 30114   LH, MI, PS, RC

404-479-3090   Type: PL   Geographical Area: Appalachia
Dorothy G. Hales, Director   Dates: 1801 to date
Mon.-Fri. 8:30-5:30; Sat. 9-4   Size: 51-150 linear feet

12 **Southeastern Railway & Museum**   Records: MS, PH, IA
National Railway Historical Society
3966 Buford Highway   Subjects: BI, CW, LA, TT
Duluth, GA 30136

404-476-2013   Type: HS   Geographical Area: Appalachia &
Michael Cosgrove, President   United States
By Appointment Only   Dates: 1861 to date
                                             Size: 151-300 linear feet

---

13 **Vann House Historic Site**   Records: MS, OH, GE, PH, IA
GA Dept. of Natural Resources
Rt. 7, Box 235   Subjects: AG, AR, BL, BI, CR, ED, EI,
Chatsworth, GA 30705   FC, GE, IN, LH, MU, PW, PS, RT,
                                                RC, TT

404-695-2598   Type: MU   Geographical Area: Appalachia
Tim Howard, Historian   Dates: 1801 to 1860
Tues.-Sat. 9-5; Sun. 2-5:30   Size: 11-50 linear feet

Kentucky

14 **Appalachian Museum**   Records: OH, AV, PH
Berea College
P. O. Box CPO2298   Subjects: AG, AR, CR, ED, FC, HS,
Berea, KY 40404   MI, MU, RC, WO

606-986-9341   Type: MU   Geographical Area: Appalachia
John Lewis, Director   Dates: 1866 to date
Mon.-Fri. 9-5   Size: 11-50 linear feet

---

15 **Appalshop Films, Inc.**   Records: AV, PH
P. O. Box 743
Whitesburg, KY 41858   Subjects: MI, WO

606-633-5708   Type: OT   Geographical Area: Appalachia
Laura Schuster   Dates: 1969 to date
By Appointment Only   Size:

---

16 **Ashland Public Library**   Records: MS, PH
1740 Central Ave.
Ashland, KY 41101   Subjects: FC, BI

606-329-0090   Type: PL   Geographical Area: Appalachia
Jim Powers, Assistant Librarian   Dates:
Mon.-Fri. 9-9; Sat. 9-6   Size: 51 linear feet

17 **Cumberland Gap Nat. Hist. Park**
P. O. Box 1848
Middlesboro, KY 40965

Records: MS, OH, AV, PH, IA
Subjects: AG, AR, BL, BI, CW, CR,
  ED, FC, GE, IN, LI, LH, MI, MU,
  NR, PA, PW, PS, PN, RT, RC, SA,
  ST, TT, WO

606-248-2817   Type:MU
Wesley D. Leishman
Mon.-Fri. 8-5

Geographical Area: Appalachia
Dates: Pre- 1800 to 1950
Size: 51-150 linear feet

18 **Eastern Kentucky Univ. Archives**
Eastern Kentucky University
Cammack Bldg., Room 26
Richmond, KY 40475

Records: MS, OH, AV, PH, IA

Subjects: BL, BI, CW, ED, FC, GE,
  HS, LI, LH, NR, PS, PN, RT, RC,
  SA, ST, WO

606-622-2820   Type: CU
Charles Hay, Archivist
Mon.-Fri. 8-4:30

Geographical Area: Appalachia
Dates: Pre-1800 to date
Size: 300-999 linear feet

19 **Greenup Co. Public Library**
203 Harrison St.
Greenup, KY 41144

Records: OH, GE, PH

Subjects: CW, ED, GE, IN, LI, LH, TT

606-473-6514   Type: PL
Dorothy K. Griffith
Mon., Tues., Thurs., Fri. 9-5; Wed. 9-8;
  Sat. 9-2

Geographical Area: Appalachia
Dates: Pre-1800 to date
Size:

20 **Harlan County Genealogical Society**
P. O. Box 1498
Harlan, KY 40831

Records: MS, OH, GE, AV, PH

Subjects: CW, FC, GE, LH, MH

                      Type: GE
Holly Fee, President
By Mail Only

Geographical Area: Appalachia
Dates: Pre-1800 to 1900
Size: 11-50 linear feet

21 **Harlan County Public Library**
Third and Central St.
Harlan, KY 40831

Records: MS, OH, GE, PH

Subjects: FC, GE, LH

606-573-5220   Type: PL
Thelma Creech
Wed., Fri., Sat. 9-5; Tues., Thur. 9-8

Geographical Area: Appalachia
Dates: 1801 to date
Size: 51-150 linear feet

22 **Henderson Settlement Mission**
United Meth. Church Project
Box 205
Frakes, KY 40940

Records: MS, OH, AV, PH

Subjects: ED, FC, LH, RC

606-337-3613   Type: CS
David L. Allen, Executive Director
Mon.-Fri. 8-4

Geographical Area: Appalachia
Dates: 1901 to date
Size: 1-10 linear feet

23 Hunt-Morgan House

Blue Grass Trust for Hist. Pres.
201 North Mill St.
Lexington, KY 40508

606-253-0362   Type: MU
Raines Taylor, Administrator
By Appointment Only

Records: MS, OH, GE, AV, PH, IA

Subjects: AG, AR, BL, BI, CW, CR,
     ED, FC, GE, HS, LA, LI, LH, MC,
     MH, MU, PA, PW, PS, PN, RT, RC,
     SA, ST, TT, WO

Geographical Area: Appalachia
Dates: Pre-1800 to date
Size: 51-150 linear feet

24 Jenkins Public Library

Jenkins, KY 41537

606-832-4101   Type: PL
Mary J. Wolfe

Records: PH

Subjects: BI, LH, MI

Geographical Area: Appalachia
Dates: 1910 to date
Size: 1-10 linear feet

25 Johnson County Public Library

P. O. Box 788
Paintsville, KY 41240

606-789-4355   Type: PL
Patricia Patton, Librarian
Mon., Wed., Fri. 9:30-5; Tues., Thurs.
     9:30-8; Sat. 9-2

Records: MS, OH, GE, PH

Subjects: CW, ED, FC, GE, LH, MI,
     PW, PS

Geographical Area: Appalachia
Dates: Pre-1800 to date
Size: 51-150 linear feet

26 KY Dept. of Mines and Minerals

120 Graham Ave.
Lexington, KY 40506

606-257-8818   Type: OT
John K. Hiett, Geologist
Mon.-Fri. 8-4:30

Records: Maps

Subjects: MI

Geographical Area: Appalachia
Dates: Pre-1800 to date
Size: 300-999 linear feet

27 Laurel County Library

116 East 4th St.
London, KY 40741

606-864-5759   Type: PL
Gladys Brewer, Asst. Librarian
Mon., Tues., Wed.,Fri. 9-6; Sat. 9-5

Records: MS, OH, GE, AV, PH

Subjects: LH

Geographical Area: Appalachia
Dates: Pre-1800 to date
Size:

28 Lexington Public Library

251 West 2nd St.
Lexington, KY 40507

606-253-1750   Type: PL
Carol J. Nicholas, Librarian
Mon.-Thurs. 9-9; Fri. & Sat. 9-5; Sun. 1-5

Records: PH, IA

Subjects: LH

Geographical Area: Appalachia
Dates: 1901 to 1950
Size: 1-10 linear feet

29 No Entry

---

30 Middlesboro-Bell County Public Library
126 South 20th St.
Middlesboro, KY 40965

Records: MS, OH, GE, PH

Subjects: BI, GE, LH

606-248-4812   Type: PL
Virginia T. Green, Director
Mon.-Fri. 10-7; Sat. 9-2

Geographical Area: Appalachia
Dates: 1866 to date
Size: 11-50 linear feet

---

31 O'rear Robinson Library
Pikeville College Media Center
Sycamore St.
Pikeville, KY 41501

Records: MS, GE, PH, IA

Subjects: ED, FC, GE, LI, LH, RC

606-432-9371   Type: CU
James M. McKellogg, Director
Sun. 3-9:30; Mon.-Tues. 8-9:30; Fri. 8-4

Geographical Area: Appalachia
Dates: 1866 to date
Size: 11-50 linear feet

---

32 Owsley Co. Historical Society
KY. Dept. for Libraries
P. O. Box 176
Booneville, KY 41314

Records: MS, GE

Subjects: GE, RC

606-593-5700   Type: PL
Joyce Marcum, Librarian
Mon.-Fri. 9-5

Geographical Area: Appalachia
Dates: Pre-1800 to date
Size: 1-10 linear feet

---

33 Perry County Genealogical and Historical Society
301 Kentucky Blvd.
Hazard, KY 41701

Records: MS, GE

Subjects: GE, LH

606-436-3864   Type: PL
Mrs. Bruce Stephens, Board
Mon.-Fri. 8-5; Sat. 8-2

Geographical Area: Appalachia
Dates:
Size:

---

34 Pike Co. Historical Society
P. O. Box 752
Pikeville, KY 41501

Records: MS, OH, GE, PH

Subjects: AR, BI, CW, ED, FC, GE, LI, LH, MI, RC

606-437-4967   Type: HS
Dorcas M. Hobbs
By Appointment Only

Geographical Area: Appalachia
Dates: Pre-1800 to date
Size: 11-50 linear feet

---

35 **Pine Mt. Settlement School**
E. J. Carr
Plant Studies Center
Pine Mountain, KY 40810

606-558-4361   Type: OT
Ellwood J. Carr
By Appointment Only

Records: MS, OH, PH

Subjects: LH, NR, RC, ST

Geographical Area: Appalachia, Eastern
    United States
Dates:
Size: 151-300 linear feet

36 **Pineville-Bell County Public
Library**
Tennessee and Walnut Sts.
Pineville, KY 40977

606-337-3422   Type: PL
Virginia Green, Director
Mon. 11-7; Tues.-Fri. 9:45-5:15; Sat. 9-1

Records: OH, GE, PH

Subjects: GE, LH

Geographical Area: Appalachia
Dates: 1866 to date
Size: 1-10 linear feet

37 **Rockcastle Co. Public Library**
Ford Dr.
Mount Vernon, KY 40456

606-256-2388   Type: PL
Alleyne Davis, Librarian
Mon., Tues., Wed., Fri. 1-5; Thurs. 1-8;
    Sat. 8:30-4

Records: OH, GE

Subjects: GE

Geographical Area: Appalachia
Dates:
Size: 1-10 linear feet

38 **Special Collections**
Berea College
Hutchins Library
Berea, KY 40404

606-986-9311   Type: CU
Charles Robb, Archivist
Mon.-Fri. 9-12, 1-4:30; Wed. 6-10 p.m.

Records: MS, OH, GE, AV, PH, IA

Subjects: AG, AR, BL, BI, CW,
    CR, ED, FC, GE, HS, LA, LI,
    LH, MI, MU, NR, PA, PS, PN,
    RC, SA, TT, WO

Geographical Area: Appalachia
Dates: 1801 to date
Size: Over 1000 linear feet

39 **Special Collections & Archives**
University of Kentucky
Univ. of Kentucky Libraries
Lexington, KY 40506

606-257-8611   Type: CU
Anne G. Campbell, Curator
Mon.-Fri. 8-4:30; Sat. 8-12; Sun. 2-5

Records: MS, OH, GE, AV, PH, IA

Subjects: AG, AR, BL, BI, CW, CR,
    ED, EI, FC, GE, HS, LA, LI, LH,
    MH, MI, MU, NR, PA, PW, PS, PN,
    RT, RC, SA, ST, TT, WO

Geographical Area: Appalachia
Dates: Pre-1800 to date
Size: Over 1000 linear feet

40 **Transylvania Univ. Library**   Records: MS, PH, IA
Transylvania University
300 North Broadway   Subjects: AG, BI, HS, LH, PW
Lexington, KY 40508

606-233-8227   Type: CU   Geographical Area: Appalachia
Kathleen C. Bryson, Curator   Dates: Pre-1800 to date
Mon.-Fri. 8:30-4   Size: 151-300 linear feet

41 **United Methodist Church**   Records: MS, OH, AV
Archives and History
1387 New Circle Rd., NE   Subjects: BL, RC
Lexington, KY 40505

606-254-7388   Type: OT   Geographical Area: Appalachia
Adrian J. Roberts, Director   Dates: 1801 to date
Mon.-Fri. 8:30-4:30   Size: 151-300 linear feet

North Carolina

42 **Alleghany Historical-Genealogical** Records: OH, GE
Society, Inc.
P. O. Box 817   Subjects: GE, LH
Sparta, NC 28675

919-372-8864   Type: PL   Geographical Area: Appalachia
Lou Reid Landreth, Secretary   Dates:
Mon.-Fri. 9-5; Sat. 9-1   Size:

43 **Appalachian Room Special**   Records: MS, OH, GE, AV, PH, IA
Collections
Mars Hill College   Subjects: AG, BL, BI, CW, CR, ED,
Mars Hill, NC 28754   FC, GE, IN, LI, LH, MU, RC

704-689-1394   Type: CU   Geographical Area: Appalachia
Richard Dillingham, Director   Dates: 1801 to date
Mon.-Fri. 12-4   Size: 151-300 linear feet

44 **Ashe County Public Library**   Records: OH, GE, PH
Appalachian Regional Library
Route 1, 148 Library Dr.   Subjects: AG, AR, BL, BI, CW, ED,
West Jefferson, NC 28694   EI, FC, GE, IN, LA, LH, MH, MI,
                                            MU, PW, PS, RC, SA, TT, WO

919-246-2041   Type: PL   Geographical Area: Appalachia
Jo Greene, Librarian   Dates: Pre-1800 to date
Mon.-Fri. 8-5; Sat. 8-3:30   Size: 51-150 linear feet

45 Asheville-Buncombe Library Sys.
Pack Memorial & Admin. Office
67 Haywood St.
Asheville, NC 28801

704-252-8701   Type: PL
John Toms, Curator
Mon.-Fri. 10-9; Sat. 10-6

Records: MS, PH, IA

Subjects: AR, CW, LI, LH, MU, NR,
   PA, RT

Geographical Area: Appalachia
Dates: 1866 to 1950
Size:

---

46 Blue Ridge Parkway
National Park Service
700 Northwestern Bank Bldg.
Asheville, NC 28401

704-259-0769   Type: OT
Steve Beatty
By Appointment Only

Records: MS, OH, PH

Subjects: AG, CR, LH, NR, PN, RC

Geographical Area: Appalachia
Dates: 1901 to date
Size: 11-50 linear feet

---

47 Broad River Genealogical Soc.
P. O. Box 2261
Shelby, NC 28150

                                Type: OT
Clara H. Hughes
By Appointment Only

Records: MS, GE, PH

Subjects: GE

Geographical Area: Appalachia
Dates:
Size: 1-10 linear feet

---

48 Burke County Public Library
204 South King St.
Morganton, NC 28655

704-437-5638   Type: PL
Scott A. Oxford, Curator
Mon.-Sat. 8:30-5:30

Records: MS, OH, GE

Subjects: AR, BL, BI, CW, ED, FC,
   GE, IN, LH, MH, MI, NR, PW, PS,
   RC, WO

Geographical Area: Appalachia
Dates: Pre-1800 to date
Size: 51-150 linear feet

---

49 Caldwell County Public Library
606 College Ave., SW
Lenoir, NC 28645

704-758-1369   Type: PL
Karen B. Doll, Librarian
Mon., Wed., Fri. 8:30-5:30; Tues.,
   Thurs. 8:30-8

Records: MS, GE

Subjects: CW, FC, GE, LH

Geographical Area: Appalachia
Dates: Pre-1800 to date
Size: 51-150 linear feet

---

50 Canton Public Library
Branch of Haywood County Lib.
36 Park St.
Canton, NC 28716

704-648-2924   Type: PL
Nan Williamson, Librarian
Mon., Wed., Fri. 9-6; Tues. 9-7:30; Sat. 9-5

Records: OH, AV, PH

Subjects: FC, LH

Geographical Area: Appalachia
Dates: 1866 to date
Size:

51 **Carl Sandburg Nat. Hist. Site**   Records: MS, OH, PH
National Park Service
P. O. Box 395   Subjects: AG, AR, BI, CW, ED, EI,
Flat Rock, NC 28731   LA, LI, MU, PN

704-693-4178   Type: MU   Geographical Area:
Warren Weber, Curator   Dates: 1861 to date
Daily 9-5   Size: 300-999 linear feet

---

52 **Catawba County Hist. Museum**   Records: MS, GE, AV, PH, IA
Catawba County Hist. Assoc.
P. O. Box 73, 1716 South College   Subjects: AG, AR, BL, BI, CW, CR,
Newton, NC 28658   ED, EI, FC, GE, IN, LI, LH, MH,
                                                  MU, PW, PS, RC, TT, WO

704-465-0383   Type: HS   Geographical Area: Appalachia
Sidney Halma   Dates: 1801 to 1950
Tue.-Fri. 9-5; Sat.-Sun. 1-5   Size: 51-150 linear feet

---

53 **Cherokee County Hist. Museum**   Records: OH, PH
205 Peachtree St.
Murphy, NC 28906   Subjects: AG, BL, ED, FC, IN, LH,
                                                  RC, TT, WO

704-837-6792   Type: HS   Geographical Area: Appalachia
Alice White, Director   Dates: 1801 to 1860; 1866 to 1950
Mon.-Fri. 9-5   Size: 1-10 linear feet

---

54 **Coweeta Hydrologic Laboratory**   Records: MS, PH
Southeastern Forest Exp. Sta.
Route 1, Box 216   Subjects: NR, ST
Otto, NC 28763

704-524-2128   Type: OT   Geographical Area: Appalachia
Dr. W. T. Swank, Project Leader   Dates: 1901 to date
Mon.-Fri. 7:30-4   Size: 1-10 linear feet

---

55 **Cradle of Forestry in America**   Records: MS, OH, AV, PH
U. S. Forest Service
P. O. Box 8   Subjects: ED, LH, NR
Pisgah Forest, NC 28768

704-877-3265   Type: MU   Geographical Area: Appalachia; United
Don Fisher, CFA Director   States; Foreign
By Appointment Only   Dates: 1866 to 1950
                                               Size: 51-150 linear feet

56 **D. D. Dougherty Library**
Appalachian State University
Room 212
Boone, NC 28608

704-262-4040   Type: CU
Michael E. Holland, Director
Mon.-Fri. 8-5

Records: MS, IA

Subjects: ED, LH, PS

Geographical Area: Appalachia
Dates: 1901 to date
Size: Over 1000 linear feet

---

57 **Davie County Public Library**
371 North Main St., Courier 531
Mocksville, NC 27028

704-634-2023   Type: PL
Ruth A. Hoyle, Director
Mon., Thurs. 9-8:30; Tues., Wed.,
   Fri. 9-5:50; Sat. 9-2

Records: MS, OH

Subjects: AG, BL, BI, CW, ED, GE,
   LH, NR, RC

Geographical Area: Appalachia
Dates: Pre-1800 to date
Size: 51-150 linear feet

---

58 **Dry Ridge Historical Museum**
North Buncombe Library
Weaverville, NC 28787

704-645-6555   Type: MU
Josephine Osborne
Sat. 11-3, By Appointment

Records: MS, GE, PH

Subjects: AG, AR, BL, BI, CW, CR,
   ED, FC, GE, IN, LA, LI, LH, MU,
   PW, RC, WO

Geographical Area: Appalachia
Dates: Pre-1800 to date
Size: 151-300 linear feet

---

59 **Eastern Cabarrus Hist. Society**
North Main St.
Mount Pleasant, NC 28124

704-436-6612   Type: MU
Billie McAllister
By Appointment Only

Records: MS, PH, IA

Subjects: CW, ED, FC, GE, IN, LH,
   MH, MU, RC

Geographical Area: Appalachia
Dates: 1801 to date
Size:

---

60 **Elbert Ivey Memorial Pub. Lib.**
420 3rd Ave., NW
Hickory, NC 28601

704-322-2905   Type: PL
Robert Russell, Director
Mon.-Thurs. 9-9; Fri.-Sat. 9-5; Sun. 2-5

Records: MS, GE, PH

Subjects: GE, LH

Geographical Area: Appalachia
Dates: 1901 to date
Size:

61 **Hist. Foundation of the Presbyterian & Reformed Church**
Box 847
Montreat, NC 28757

704-669-7061 Type: OT
Jerrold Lee Brooks
Mon.-Fri. 8:30-4:30; Sat. 9-1

Records: MS, OH, GE, AV, PH, IA

Subjects: BL, CW, ED, FC, GE, IN, LH, MU, RC, SA, WO

Geographical Area: Appalachia, United States, Foreign
Dates: Pre-1800 to date
Size: Over 1000 linear feet

62 **Historic Resources Commission of Asheville & Buncombe Co.**
Room 515, City Building
Asheville, NC 28807

704-255-5434 Type: OT
Carolyn A. Humphries, Director
Tues., Wed., Thur., 9-5

Records: IA (Records on Historic Bldgs.)

Subjects: AR

Geographical Area: Appalachia
Dates: 1801 to 1950
Size:

63 **Hunter Library**
Western Carolina University
Special Collections
Cullowhee, NC 28723

704-227-7474 Type: CU
James B. Lloyd
Mon.-Fri. 8-12; 1-5

Records: MS, GE, AV, PH, IA

Subjects: BL, BI, CW, ED, FC, GE, HS, IN, LI, LH, MI, NR, PA, PS, PN, RT, RC, WO

Geographical Area: Appalachia, United States
Dates: Pre-1800 to date
Size: 300-999 linear feet

64 **Jacob S. Mauney Mem. Library**
100 South Piedmont
Kings Mountain, NC 28086

704-739-2371 Type: PL
Rose Turner, Director
Mon. 12-8; Tue.-Sat. 10-6

Records: GE

Subjects: GE

Geographical Area: Appalachia
Dates:
Size: 1-10 linear feet

65 **James Larkin Pearson Library**
Wilkes Community College
Box 120
Wilkesboro, NC 28667

919-696-4465 Type: OT
Fay Byrd, Director
By Appointment Only

Records: MS, OH, AV, PH

Subjects:

Geographical Area: Appalachia
Dates: 1901 to 1950
Size:

66 **Macon County Public Library**
Fontana Regional Library
45 Wayah St.
Franklin, NC 28734

704-524-3600   Type: PL
Cynthia Modlin, Librarian
Mon., Wed., Fri., Sat. 10-5:30;
    Tues., Thurs. 10-9

Records: MS

Subjects: GE, LH

Geographical Area: Appalachia
Dates: 1801 to date
Size: 1-10 linear feet

67 **Mayland Technical College**
P. O. Box 547
Spruce Pine, NC 28777

704-765-7351   Type: CU
Kenneth Nelson, Faculty
Mon.-Thurs. 8-9:30; Fri. 8-8

Records: MS, OH, GE

Subjects: AG, BI, CW, CR, EI, FC, GE,
    LH, MI

Geographical Area: Appalachia
Dates: Pre-1800 to date
Size: 151-300 linear feet

68 **Moravian Archives**
Moravian Church in America
Drawer M, Salem Station
Winston-Salem, NC 27101

919-722-1742   Type:CS
Mary Creech, Archivist
Mon.-Fri. 9-4:30

Records: IA

Subjects: RC

Geographical Area: Appalachia
Dates:
Size:

69 **Moravian Music Foundation**
20 Cascade Ave.
Winston-Salem, NC 27107

919-725-0651   Type: CS
James Boeninger
Mon.-Fri. 9-4

Records: MS, GE, AV, PH, IA

Subjects: AR, CW, ED, FC, GE, IN, LI,
    LH, MU, PW, RC, WO

Geographical Area: Appalachia,
    Pennsylvania, Ohio, Germany
Dates: Pre-1800 to date
Size:

70 **Museum of the Cherokee Indian**
Drama Rd.
U. S. Highway 441 North
Cherokee, NC 28719

704-497-3481   Type: MU
Maxine F. Hill, Manager
By Appointment Only

Records: MS, PH

Subjects: BI, CR, ED, EI, FC, IN, LH,
    MU, PS, RT

Geographical Area: Appalachia
Dates: 1861 to date
Size: 151-300 linear feet

71 **Museum of Waldensian History**
Waldensian Presbyterian Church
Rodoret St.
Valdese, NC 28690

704-874-2531   Type: MU
Paul H. Felker, Minister
By Appointment Only

Records: OH, GE, PH

Subjects: EI, GE

Geographical Area: Appalachia
Dates: 1866 to 1950
Size: 1-10 linear feet

72 **N. C. Baptist Hist. Collection**
Wake Forest University
Z. Smith Reynolds Library
Winston-Salem, NC 27109

919-761-5472   Type: CU
John R. Woodard, Director
Mon.-Fri. 8:30-4:30

Records: MS, OH, GE, AV, PH, IA

Subjects: AG, AR, BL, BI, CW, ED,
FC, GE, IN, LA, LI, LH, MH, MI,
MU, PS, PN, RC, ST, TT, WO

Geographical Area: Appalachia, North
Carolina, Foreign
Dates: Pre-1800 to date
Size: 300-999 linear feet

73 **National Forests in NC**
U. S. Forest Service
50 South Broad St.
Asheville, NC 28802

704-253-1636   Type: OT
W. W. Rule, Public Affairs
Mon.-Fri. 8-5

Records: MS, OH, AV, PH, IA

Subjects: AG, BI, ED, NR, RT, TT

Geographical Area: National Forests,
North Carolina
Dates: 1901 to date
Size: 51-150 linear feet

74 **Old Buncombe Co. Genealogical
Society, Inc.**
44 Haywood St.
Asheville, NC 28801

704-253-1894   Type: GE
Doris A. Cline Ward, Secretary
Mon.-Fri. 9-5

Records: MS, GE

Subjects: BL,CW, EI, GE, IN, LH

Geographical Area: Appalachia, United
States, Foreign
Dates: Pre-1800 to date
Size: 151-300 linear feet

75 **Polk County Historical
Association's Museum**
1 Depot St.
Tryon, NC 28782

704-894-8827   Type: HS
J. C. Placak, Jr., Curator
Tues., Thurs. 10-12

Records: MS, AV, PH, IA

Subjects: AG, AR, BL, CW, FC, GE
IN, LI, LH, MH, MI, PS, RC

Geographical Area: Appalachia
Dates: 1901 to 1950
Size: 11-50 linear feet

76 **Thomas Wolfe Memorial**
NC Dept. of Cultural Resources
48 Spruce St.
Asheville, NC 28801

704-253-8304   Type: MU
Steve Hill, Manager
Mon.-Sat. 9-5; Sun. 1-5

Records: MS, OH, GE, AV, PH, IA

Subjects: FC, GE, LI, LH, MU

Geographical Area: Appalachia,
     Pennsylvania, New York
Dates: 1866 to 1950
Size: 51-150 linear feet

77 **Transylvania County Library**
105 S. Broad St.
Brevard, NC 28712

704-884-3151   Type: PL
Roberta S. Williams, Director

Records: MS, GE, PH

Subjects: AG, AR, BL, BI, CW, CR,
     ED, EI, FC, GE, HS, IN, LA, LI, LH,
     MC, MH, MI, MU, NR, PA, PW, PS,
     PN, RT, RC, SA, ST, TT, WO

Geographical Area: Appalachia
Dates: Pre-1800 to date
Size: 51-150 linear feet

78 **University Archives**
Wake Forest University
P. O. Box 7777
Winston-Salem, NC 27109

919-761-5472   Type: CU
Myrtle Little, Assistant
Mon.-Fri. 8:30-4:30

Records: MS, OH, AV, PH, IA

Subjects: FC, PS, PN, RC

Geographical Area: United States
Dates: 1801 to 1860
Size:

79 **W. L. Eury Appalachian Collect.**
Appalachian State University
University Hall
Boone, NC 28608

704-262-4041   Type: CU
Eric J. Olson, Librarian
Mon.-Thurs. 8-9; Fri. 8-5; Sat. 9-1;
     Sun. 5-9

Records: MS, OH, GE, AV, PH

Subjects: AG, AR, BL, BI, CW, CR,
     ED, EI, FC, GE, HS, IN, LA, LI, LH,
     MC, MH, MI, MU, NR, PA, PW, PS,
     RT, RC, SA, ST, TT, WO

Geographical Area: Appalachia
Dates: Pre-1800 to date
Size: 151-300 linear feet

80 **Yadkin Historical Society**
Yadkin County Library
Yadkinville, NC 27055

           Type: HS
Irma Robertson, Member

Records: MS, GE

Subjects: AG, CW, ED, FC, GE, LH,
     MH, RC, TT, WO

Geographical Area: Appalachia
Dates: Pre-1800 to 1950
Size: 11-50 linear feet

81 **Zebulon B. Vance Birthplace**   Records: MS, GE, AV
NC Dept. of Archives & History
911 Reems Creek Rd.   Subjects: CW, CR, GE, LH
Weaverville, NC 28787

704-645-6706   Type: MU   Geographical Area: Appalachia
Sudie Wheeler, Manager   Dates: 1801 to 1860
Mon.-Sat. 9-5, Sun. 1-5   Size: 11-50 linear feet

South Carolina

82 **Greenville County**   Records: MS, AV, PH, IA
   Historical Society
   Greenville County Library   Subjects: AR, BI, CW, ED, FC, GE, LI,
   300 College St.   LH, PS, WO
   Greenville, SC 29601

   803-242-5000   Type: PL   Geographical Area: Appalachia
   Steve Richardson, Archivist   Dates: 1801 to date
   Mon.-Fri. 9-9; Sat. 9-6; Sun. 2-6   Size: 11-50 linear feet

83 **Oconee County Library**   Records: MS, GE, PH
   301 S. Spring St.
   Walhalla, SC 29691   Subjects: GE, FC, LH

   803-638-5837   Type: PL   Geographical Area: Appalachia
   Dorothy Chandler, Director   Dates: Pre-1800 to date
   Mon.-Tues. 9-9; Wed.-Fri. 9-6; Sat. 9-1   Size:

84 **Pendleton Dist. Hist. &**   Records: MS, OH, GE, PH, IA
   Rec. Comm.
   P. O. Box 565   Subjects: AG, BL, BI, CW, FC, GE,
   Pendleton, SC 29670   LA, LH, RT, RC

   803-646-3782   Type: OT   Geographical Area: Appalachia
   Donna Roper, Archivist   Dates: Pre-1800 to date
   Mon.-Fri. 9-4:30   Size: 51-150 linear feet

85 **Pickens Co. Hist. Society**   Records: MS, PH
   Johnson and Pendleton
   Pickens, SC 29671   Subjects: AG, CW, ED, FC, IN, LH,
                                                   PS, RC

   803-878-7818   Type: HS   Geographical Area: Appalachia
   Dorothy Blase   Dates: Pre-1800 to date
   Mon. 2-5; Wed. 9-12; Thurs. 9-12 &   Size: Over 1000 linear feet
     1-4; Fri. 2-5

86 **Pickens County Library**
110 W. First Ave.
Easley, SC 29640

803-859-9679   Type: PL
Penny Forrester, Director
Mon. 9-9; Tues.-Fri. 9-6; Sat. 9-4

Records: MS, OH, PH, IA

Subjects: FC, GE, LH

Geographical Area: Appalachia
Dates: 1901 to date
Size: 11-50 linear feet

---

87 **Special Collections**
Robert Muldrow Cooper Library
Clemson University
Clemson, SC 29631

803-656-3031   Type: CU
Michael Kohl
Mon., Wed., Thurs., Fri. 8-4:30;
  Tues. 8-9

Records: MS, GE, AV, PH, IA

Subjects: AG, BL, BI, ED, GE, LI, LH,
  MH, NR, PS, PN, ST

Geographical Area: Appalachia
Dates: Pre-1800 to date
Size: Over 1000 linear feet

---

88 **Special Collections/Archives**
Furman University Library
Furman University
Greenville, SC 29613

803-294-2194   Type: CU
J. Glenwood Clayton, Archivist
Mon.-Fri. 8:30-4:30

Records: MS, OH, GE, AV, PH, IA

Subjects: CW, ED, FC, GE, LI, MU,
  RC

Geographical Area: Appalachia,
  South Carolina
Dates: Pre-1800 to date
Size:

Tennessee

89 **Andrew Johnson National
Historical Site**
U. S. National Park Service
College & Depot Sts. Box 1088
Greenville, TN 37744

615-638-3551
Ed Speer, Park Technician
Mon.-Sun. 9-5

Records: MS, OH, GE, AV, PH, IA

Subjects: CW, GE, LH, PS, PN

Geographical Area: Appalachia,
  Washington, D.C.
Dates: Pre-1800 to date
Size: 1-10 linear feet

---

90 **Archives and Special Cols.**
Carson-Newman College Library
Russell St.
Jefferson City, TN 37760

615-475-9061   Type: CU
Imogene Brewer
Mon.-Fri. 8:30-5

Records: MS, PH

Subjects: CW, ED, FC, GE, LH, RC,
  WO

Geographical Area: Appalachia
Dates: 1861 to 1865
Size: 1-10 linear feet

91 **Archives of Appalachia**
East Tennessee State University
Sherrod Library
Johnson City, TN 37614

615-929-4338   Type: CU
Ellen Garrison, Director
Mon.-Fri. 8-4:30

Records: MS, OH, GE, AV, PH, IA

Subjects: AG, AR, BL, BI, CW, CR,
ED, FC, GE, HS, LA, LI, LH, MC,
MI, MU, NR, PA, PS, PN, RC, SA,
ST, TT, WO

Geographical Area: Appalachia
Dates: Pre-1800 to date
Size: Over 1000 linear feet

92 **Bradley County
Historical Society**
P. O. Box 2424
Cleveland, TN 37320

615-476-2921   Type: HS
Bill Snell
Mon.-Sat. 9-5

Records: MS, OH, GE, PH, IA

Subjects: BL, BI, CW, ED, FC, GE, IN,
LA, LH, NR, PS, RC

Geographical Area: Appalachia
Dates: 1801 to date
Size: 151-300 linear feet

93 **Calvin M. McClung
Collection**
Knox County Public Library
600 Market St.
Knoxville, TN 37902

615-523-0781   Type: PL
W. J. MacArthur
Mon.-Tues. 9-8; Wed.-Fri. 9-5:30

Records: MS, OH, GE, AV, PH, IA

Subjects: AG, AR, BL, BI, CW, CR,
ED, EI, FC, GE, HS, IN, LA, LI, LH,
MC, MH, MI, MU, NR, PA, PW, PS,
PN, RT, RC, SA, ST, TT, WO

Geographical Area: Appalachia,
United States, Foreign
Dates: Pre-1800 to date
Size: Over 1000 linear feet

94 **Carroll Reece Museum**
East Tennessee State University
P. O. Box 22300A
Johnson City, TN 37614

615-929-4392   Type: MU
Helen Roseberry, Director
Mon.-Fri. 9-4; Sat., Sun. 1-5

Records: MS, GE, AV, PH, IA

Subjects: AR, BI, CW, FC, GE, LH,
MH, MI, MU, PS, PN, RT, RC,
ST, WO

Geographical Area: Appalachia,
United States; Foreign
Dates: 1866 to date
Size: 151-300 linear feet

95 **Children's Museum of Oak Ridge**
461 West Outer Dr.
P. O. Box 3066
Oak Ridge, TN 37830

615-482-2215   Type: MU
Jane Barnes Alderfer
Mon.-Fri. 9-12 or by Appointment

Records: MS, OH, AV, PH
Subjects: AG, AR, BL, BI, CW, CR,
ED, EI, FC, GE, HS, IN, LA, LI, LH,
MH, MI, MU, NR, PA, PW, PS, PN,
RT, RC, SA, ST, TT, WO

Geographical Area: Appalachia
Dates: Pre-1800 to date
Size: 151-300 linear feet

96 Cleveland State Community College Library
Box 3570
Cleveland, TN 37311

615-472-7141   Type: CU
Adeline Baskett, Librarian

Records: MS

Subjects: FC, LH, RC

Geographical Area: Appalachia
Dates: 1980 to 1860
Size: 1-10 linear feet

---

97 Dayton Library
South Market St.
Dayton, TN 37321

615-775-9063   Type: PL
Tennga S. Conner

Records: AV

Subjects: GE, LH

Geographical Area: Appalachia
Dates: 1801 to 1950
Size: 1-10 linear feet

---

98 Dulin Gallery of Art
3100 Kingston Pike
Knoxville, TN 37919

615-525-6101   Type: MU
Paul Wenzel

Records: PH

Subjects: AR

Geographical Area: Appalachia
Dates: Pre-1800
Size: 300-999 linear feet

---

99 E. W. King Library
King College, Inc.
King College Rd.
Bristol, TN 37620

615-968-1187   Type: CU
Mark Y. Herring, Director
Mon.-Thurs. 8-10:30; Fri. 8 5; Add.
    Hrs.

Records: MS, OH, GE, PH, IA

Subjects: AG, AR, BL, CW, ED, FC,
    GE, LI, LH, MI, PW, PS, RC

Geographical Area: Appalachia
Dates: Pre-1800 to date

Size: 300-999 linear feet

---

100 Elizabethton Public Library
Sycamore St.
Elizabethton, TN 37643

615-542-4841   Type: PL
Joyce L. Hawthorne, Director
Mon.-Thurs. 10-8; Tues.-Fri. 10-6; Wed.
    10-12; Sat. 10-4

Records: GE

Subjects: GE, LH

Geographical Area: Appalachia
Dates: 1866 to date

Size: 1-10 linear feet

---

101 Fort Sanders Regional Medical Center—Nursing Library
1915 White Ave.
Knoxville, TN 37916

615-971-1293   Type: OT
Nedra Cook, Librarian
Mon. 8-7; Tues.-Fri. 8-4:30

Records: PH, IA

Subjects: ED, FC, HS, LH, ST

Geographical Area: Appalachia
Dates: 1901 to date
Size: 1-10 linear feet

102 **Frank F. McClung Museum**   Records: MS, PH
University of Tennessee
Circle Park Dr.   Subjects: AG, AR, CW, CR, FC, IN,
Knoxville, TN 37996   LH, NR

615-974-2144   Type: CU   Geographical Area: Appalachia,
Jefferson Chapman, Curator   United States, Foreign
Mon.-Fri. 9-5   Dates: Pre-1800 to date
                                         Size: Over 1000 linear feet

103 **Great Smoky Mountains National**   Records: MS, OH, GE, PH, IA
Park
Gatlinburg, TN 37863   Subjects: GE, NR, PW, RT

615-436-5615   Type: OT   Geographical Area: Appalachia
Kathleen L. Manscill   Dates: 1866 to 1950
Mon.-Fri. 8-4:30   Size: 151-300 linear feet

104 **H. B. Stamps Memorial Library**   Records: GE
407 E. Main St.
Rogersville, TN 37857   Subjects: GE, LH

615-272-8710   Type: PL   Geographical Area: Appalachia
Kathy Moore, Director   Dates: Pre-1800 to date
Mon., Wed., Thurs., Fri. 9:30-5;   Size: 11-50 linear feet
   Tues. 9:30-8

105 NO ENTRY

106 **Hardwick Johnston Memorial**   Records: MS, PH, IA
Library
Hiwassee College   Subjects: LH, RC
Madisonville, TN 37354

615-442-3343   Type: CU   Geographical Area: Appalachia
Kent Millwood, Librarian   Dates: 1801 to date
Mon.-Fri. 8-5   Size: 51-150 linear feet

107 NO ENTRY

108 Kingsport Public Library   Records: OH, GE
Broad & New Sts.
Kingsport, TN 37660   Subjects: GE, LH

615-245-3141   Type: PL   Geographical Area: Appalachia
Dorothy D. Knierim   Dates: 1901 to date
Mon.-Fri. 9-6   Size: 1-10 linear feet

109 NO ENTRY

110 **Merner-Pfeiffer Library**
Tennessee Wesleyan College
Box 40
Athens, TN 37303

615-745-2363   Type: CU
James D. Tingen

Records: MS, IA

Subjects: CW, LH, RC

Geographical Area: Appalachia
Dates: 1861 to date
Size: 11-50 linear feet

111 **Morristown Hamblen Library**
417 West Main St.
Morristown, TN 37814

615-586-6410   Type: PL
Polly Potter, Director
Mon., Wed., Fri., Sat. 9:30-5:30;
  Tues., Thurs. 9:30-8

Records: MS, IA

Subjects: EI, GE, LH, RC

Geographical Area: Appalachia
Dates: Pre-1800 to 1950
Size: 151-300 linear feet

112 **Norris Dam State Park**
Will G. & Helen H. Lenoir Museum
Box 53
Norris, TN 37828

615-494-7673   Type: MU
Betty Lovell
Summer: Every Day; Winter: Sat., Sun.

Records: MS

Subjects: BL, BI, CW, ED, GE, LH,
  MI, PW, PS, SA

Geographical Area: Appalachia
Dates: Pre-1800 to 1950
Size:

113 **Oak Ridge Public Library**
Civic Center
Oak Ridge, TN 37830

615-483-6386   Type: PL
Dorothy B. Diemuke
Mon.-Thurs. 10-9; Fri. 10-6; Sat. 9-6;
  Sun. 2-6

Records: MS, OH, AV, PH

Subjects: LH

Geographical Area: Appalachia
Dates:
Size:

114 **P. H. Welshimer Memorial
Library**
Milligan College
Milligan College, TN 37682

615-929-0116   Type: CU
Billie B. Oakes, Assistant Librarian
Mon.-Fri. 8-5

Records: MS, PH, IA

Subjects: ED, RC

Geographical Area: Appalachia
Dates: 1866 to date
Size: 11-50 linear feet

115 **Parrott-Wood Library**
Branch of Jefferson County Library
Old Andrew Johnson Highway
Strawberry Plains, TN 37871

615-933-1311   Type: PL
Wenona H. McBee, Librarian
Mon.-Wed. 1-6; Thurs. 2-6; Fri. 10-2

Records: MS, PH

Subjects: BI, CW, ED, LH, MI, PS, RC

Geographical Area: Appalachia
Dates: 1861 to date
Size: 11-50 linear feet

116 **Pentecostal Research Center**
Pentecostal Resource Center
Cleveland, TN 37311

Type: CU
Frances Arrington, Librarian
Mon. 1-9; Tues. 1-5; Wed. 8-10 & 1-9;
  Tues. 1-5; Fri. 8-12

Records: MS, OH, AV, PH, IA

Subjects: ED, FC, LH, MU, RC, WO

Geographical Area: Appalachia,
  United States, Foreign
Date: 1901 to date
Size: Over 1000 linear feet

117 **Quillen-Dishner College
of Medicine Library**
East Tennessee State University
Johnson City, TN 37614

615-928-6426   Type: CU
Martha Whaley
By Appointment Only

Records: MS, OH, AV, PH, IA

Subjects: HS

Geographical Area: Appalachia
Dates: 1901 to date
Size: 11-50 linear feet

118 **Restoration Movement Archives**
Emmanuel School of Religion
B. D. Phillips Memorial Building
Johnson City, TN 37601

615-926-1186   Type: OT
Thomas E. Stokes, Librarian
Mon.-Fri. 8-5

Records: MS, OH, AV, PH, IA

Subjects: RC

Geographical Area: Appalachia,
  United States
Dates: 1801 to date
Size: 151-300 linear feet

119 **Rose Center Museum**
442 West Second North St.
P. O. Box 1976
Morristown, TN 37814

615-581-4330   Type: MU
William Kornrich
Mon.-Fri. 11-5

Records: MS, PH

Subjects: AG, BI, ED, FC, LH, MH,
  PS, RC, TT, WO

Geographical Area: Appalachia
Dates: 1866 to date
Size 11-50 linear feet

120 NO ENTRY

121 **Special Collections Library**
University of Tennessee
University of Tennessee Library
Knoxville, TN 37996

615-974-4480   Type: CU
John Dobson
Mon.-Fri. 9-5:30

Records: MS, PH, IA

Subjects: BI, CW, ED, IN, LI, LH, MH,
  PA, PW, PS, PN, RC, ST

Geographical Area: Appalachia,
  Southern United States
Dates: Pre-1800 to date
Size: Over 1000 linear feet

122 **Speedwell Manor**
Speedwell Heritage Foundation
2112 Manor Rd.
Knoxville, TN 37920

615-577-2757   Type: MU
Virginia B. Rogers, Director
Tues., Thurs., Sun. 1-5

Records: MS, PH, IA

Subjects: BI, CW, FC, HS, LI, LH

Geographical Area: Appalachia
Dates: 1801 to 1865 & 1951 to date
Size:

123 **Sullivan County Public Library**
Box 157
205 Main St.
Blountville, TN 37617

615-323-5301   Type: PL
Roberta J. Slagle
Mon.-Sat. 9-5

Records: GE

Subjects: ED, GE, RC

Geographical Area: Appalachia
Dates: 1801 to 1950
Size: 1-10 linear feet

124 **Sycamore Shoals State Historical Area**
1615 West Elk Avenue
Elizabethton, TN 37643

615-543-5808   Type: MU
Herbert W. Roberts, Ranger
Daily 8-4:30

Records: MS, OH, PH

Subjects: AG, AR, BI, CR, ED, EI, FC, GE, IN, LA, LH, MH, MI, PW, PS, PN, RT, RC, TT, WO

Geographical Area: Appalachia
Dates: Pre-1800 to 1860
Size: 11-50 linear feet

125 **Tennessee Valley Authority**
100 Lupton Building
Chattanooga, TN 37402

615-751-2520   Type: OT
Ronald E. Brewer
Mon.-Fri. 8-4

Records: MS, OH, AV, PH

Subjects: AG, AR, BL, BI, CR, ED, FC, HS, IN, LA, MI, NR, RT, SA, ST, TT, WO

Geographical Area: Appalachia
Dates: 1901 to date
Size: 300-999 linear feet

126 **Tusculum College Library**
Tusculum College
Greenville, TN 37743

615-639-1481   Type: CU
Cleo Treadway
By Appointment Only

Records: PH, IA

Subjects: ED, LH, RC

Geographical Area: Appalachia
Dates: Pre-1800 to date
Size: 300-999 linear feet

127 **Unicoi County Historical Society**   Records: MS, OH, GE, PH
Unicoi County Library
Erwin, TN 37650   Subjects: CW, ED, FC, GE, IN, LH,
                                                     MH, PW, RC

615-743-6533   Type: HS   Geographical Area: Appalachia
Hilda Padgett, Librarian   Dates: Pre-1800 to date
Mon., Tues., Fri., Sat. 12:30-5:30;   Size: 11-50 linear feet
   Thurs. 10-5:30

128 **Veterans Administration**   Records: OH, PH, IA
Medical Center
Mountain Home, TN 37684   Subjects: AG, AR, BL, FC, HS, LH,
                                                     MH, MU, PS, RT

615-926-1171   Type: OT   Geographical Area: Appalachia
Ken Harrison   Dates: 1901 to date
By Appointment Only   Size: 11-50 linear feet

Virginia

129 **Blue Ridge Heritage Archive**   Records: MS, OH, AV, PH
Ferrum College
Blue Ridge Institute   Subjects: AG, AR, BL, BI, CR, ED, EI,
Ferrum, VA 24088   FC, LA, LH, MU, PA, RT, RC,
                                                     TT, WO

703-365-2121   Type: CU   Geographical Area: Appalachia
Vaughan Webb   Dates: 1801 to date
By Appointment Only   Size: 151-300 linear feet

130 **Buchanan County**   Records: GE, PH
Public Library
Rt. 5, Box 216   Subjects: GE
Grundy, VA 24614

703-935-2959   Type: PL   Geographical Area: Appalachia
Patricia M. Hatfield   Dates: 1861 to 1950
Mon. 1-8; Tues., Wed., Fri., Sat. 8:30-5;   Size: 11-50 linear feet
   Thurs. 8:30-8

131 **Carol M. Newman Library**   Records: MS, OH, GE, AV, PH, IA
Virginia Polytechnic Institute and
State University   Subjects: AG, BI, CW, CR, ED, FC,
Blacksburg, VA 24061   GE, LA, LI, LH, MH, MI, PW, PS,
                                                     PN, RC, ST, TT, WO

703-961-6308   Type: CU   Geographical Area: Appalachia
Glenn L. McMullen   Dates: Pre-1800 to date
Mon.-Fri. 9-4:30   Size: Over 1000 linear feet

132 Easley Library
Bluefield College
Bluefield, VA 24605

306-327-7137   Type: CU
Scott R. Johnson, Librarian
Mon.-Thurs. 8-10; Fri. 8-5

Records: IA

Subjects: ED, LH

Geographical Area: Appalachia
Dates: 1951 to date
Size: 1-10 linear feet

---

133 Fishburn Library
Hollins College
Roanoke, VA 24020

703-362-6591   Type: CU
Anthony B. Thompson
Mon.-Fri. 8:30-3:30

Records: MS, OH, GE, AV, PH, IA

Subjects: AR, BL, CW, ED, FC, GE,
LH, RC, WO

Geographical Area: Appalachia
Dates: Pre-1800 to date
Size: 300-999 linear feet

---

134 Grayson County
Historical Society
P. O. Box 529
Independence, VA 24348

703-773-2761   Type: HS
Laura Bryant, Librarian
Mon., Wed., Fri. 8-5; Tues., Thurs. 8-7;
  Sat. 10-2

Records: MS, OH, GE, PH, IA

Subjects: AG, AR, BL, BI, CW, CR,
ED, EI, FC, GE, IN, LA, LI, LH,
MU, NR, PA, PW, PS, RT, RC, ST,
TT, WO

Geographical Area: Appalachia
Dates: Pre-1800 to date
Size: 300-999 linear feet

---

135 Historical Society of
Washington County, Virginia Inc.
P. O. Box 484
Abingdon, VA 24210

            Type: HS
Mrs. Graham Landrum, President
Mon.-Fri. 10-5

Records: MS, GE, PH, IA

Subjects: AR, BI, CW, ED, FC, GE, IN,
LI, LH, MH, MI, PA, PW, PS, PN,
RT, RC, TT, WO

Geographical Area: Appalachia,
  United States
Dates: Pre-1800 to date
Size: 300-999 linear feet

---

136 Historical Crab Orchard Museum
P. O. Box 12, Route 19/460
Tazewell, VA 24651

703-988-6755   Type: MU
Nellie W. Bunoy, Director
Tues.-Sat. 10-5

Records: MS, OH, GE, PH

Subjects: AG, BL, BI, CW, CR, ED,
FC, GE, IN, LA, LI, LH, MH, MI,
MU, NR, PW, PS, PN, RT, RC,
TT, WO

Geographical Area: Appalachia,
  United States
Dates: Pre-1800 to date
Size: 51-150 linear feet

137 **Holston Conference Archives**
Kelly Library
Emory and Henry College
Emory, VA 24327

703-944-3121　　　　　　　Type CU
Maribel Elton, Archivist
Mon.-Fri. 8-5; Sat. 2-5; Sun. 8-11

Records: MS, OH, GE, PH, IA

Subjects: BL, CW, ED, EI, FC, GE, IN,
　LH, MH, PW, RC, WO

Geographical Area: Appalachia,
　United States, Foreign
Dates: Pre-1800 to date
Size: 11-50 linear feet

---

138 **John Cook Wyllie Library**
Clinch Valley College of the
University of Virginia
Wise, VA 24293

703-328-2431　　　　　　　Type: CU
Rosemary P. Mercure
Mon.-Fri. 8-4:30

Records: MS, OH, GE, PH, IA

Subjects: BI, CW, ED, FC, GE, LA,
　LH, MI, MU, NR, RC, SA

Geographical Area: Appalachia
Dates: Pre-1800 to date
Size: 300-999 linear feet

---

139 **John Preston McConnell Library**
Radford University
Radford, VA 24142

703-731-5471　　　　　　　Type: CU
Ann Swain
Mon.-Fri. 8-5

Records: MS, OH, GE, AV, PH, IA

Subjects: AG, BL, BI, CR, ED, EI, FC,
　GE, LH, MI, MU, RT, RC, TT, WO

Geographical Area: Appalachia
Dates: 1866 to date
Size: 151-300 linear feet

---

140 **Kelly Library**
Emory & Henry College
Emory, VA 24327

703-944-3121　　　　　　　Type: CU
Leroy S. Strohl, Librarian
By Appointment Only

Records: MS, OH, AV, PH, IA

Subjects: AG, BI, CW, ED, FC, LA,
　LH, MI, PS, RC, TT, WO

Geographical Area: Appalachia
Dates: 1861 to date
Size: 300-999 linear feet

---

141 **Montgomery-Floyd
Regional Library**
201 Radford St.
Christiansburg, VA 24051

703-382-3342　　　　　　　Type: PL
Kathryn I. Martens

Records: MS, PH

Subjects: LH

Geographical Area: Appalachia
Dates: 1951 to date
Size: 1-10 linear feet

142 **Patrick County Branch**
Blue Ridge Regional Library
Blue Ridge St.
Stuart, VA 24171

703-694-3352   Type: PL
Frank Quinn, Librarian
Mon., Wed., Thurs. 10-6; Tues. 10-8;
   Fri. 9-5; Sat. 9-12

Records: OH, GE, AV, PH

Subjects: AG, AR, BL, BI, CW, ED,
   FC, GE, LA, LI, LH, MU, PS, RT,
   RC, TT, WO

Geographical Area: Appalachia
Dates: Pre-1800 to date
Size: 51-150 linear feet

---

143 **Pearisburg Public Library**
112 S. Tazewell St.
Pearisburg, VA 24134

703-921-2556   Type: PL
Ruby B. Johnston, Librarian
Mon. 12-8; Tues. 1-5; Wed., Fri. 9-5;
   Thurs. 9-5 & 6-8

Records: MS, OH, GE

Subjects: AG, BL, BI, CW, CR, ED, EI,
   FC, GE, HS, IN, LA, LI, LH, MI,
   MU, NR, PA, PW, PS, RT, WO

Geographical Area: Appalachia
Dates: Pre-1800 to 1860 & 1951 to date
Size: 51-150 linear feet

---

144 **Pulaski County Library**
60 West 3rd St.
Pulaski, VA 24301

703-980-8888   Type: PL
Melinda Nurmi

Records: GE

Subjects: CW, FC, GE, LH, PS, RC

Geographical Area: Appalachia
Dates: 1801 to 1900
Size: 1-10 linear feet

---

145 **Roanoke College Library**
Roanoke College
212 High St.
Salem, VA 24153

703-389-2351   Type: CU
George Craddock, Librarian
Mon.-Thurs. 8-11; Fri. 8-5

Records: IA

Subjects:

Geographical Area: Appalachia
Dates: 1801 to date
Size: 151-300 linear feet

---

146 **Smithfield Plantation House**
Montgomery Branch of APVA
Special Collections, VPI
Blacksburg, VA 24060

703-951-2060   Type: MU
C. Leslie McCombs, Director
Mar.-Oct.: Wed., Sat., Sun. 1-5

Records: PH

Subjects: AG, AR, EI, FC, GE, IN, LH,
   MH, PW, PS, PN

Geographical Area: Appalachia
Dates:
Size:

147 **Smyth County Historical**   Records: MS, AV, PH
    Museum and Society, Inc.
    Stadium Dr.   Subjects: AG, BI, CW, CR, ED, GE,
    Marion, VA 24354   IN, LH, RC

    703-783-7674   Type: HS   Geographical Area: Appalachia
    Mack H. Sturgill   Dates: 1801 to date
    By Appointment Only   Size: 11-50 linear feet

148 **Tazewell County**   Records: GE, PH, IA
    Public Library
    310 East Main St.   Subjects: FC, GE, LH
    Tazewell, VA 24651

    703-988-2541   Type: PL   Geographical Area: Appalachia
    Laurie Surface, Director   Dates: Pre-1800 to date
    Mon., Tues., Wed., Fri. 9-5:30;   Size: 51-150 linear feet
       Thurs. 8:30; Sat. 9-5; Sun. 2-4

149 **Wilderness Rd.**   Records: MS, OH, GE, AV, PH, IA
    Regional Museum
    New River Historical Society   Subjects: AG, BI, CW, ED, FC, GE,
    P. O. Box 373   LH, MU, RC, TT
    Newbern, VA 24126

                             Type: HS   Geographical Area: Appalachia
    Mrs. Louise T. Cook, Curator   Dates: Pre-1800 to date
    Sat.-Sun. 2-5   Size: 11-50 linear feet

West Virginia

150 **Alexander Campbell Archives**   Records: MS, GE, PH, IA
    T. W. Phillips Library
    Bethany College   Subjects: ED, GE, RC
    Bethany, WV 26032

    304-829-7321   Type: CU   Geographical Area: Appalachia
    Nancy Sandercox, Head Librarian   Dates: 1801 to 1860
    Mon.-Fri. 8-4   Size: 151-300 linear feet

151 **Brooke County Historical Society**
Brooke County Public Library
1200 Pleasant Ave.
Wellsburg, WV 26070

Type: HS
Nancy L. Caldwell
Mon.-Fri. 1-9; Sat. 9-5

Records: MS, OH, GE, AV, PH

Subjects: BI, CW, ED, GE, LH, MI, RC, TT

Geographical Area: Appalachia
Dates: Pre-1800 to date
Size:

---

152 **Burnsville Public Library**
Upshur County Library
Kanawha St.
Burnsville, WV 26335

304-853-9410   Type: PL
Mary S. Black, Director
Mon.-Fri. 12-5; Sat. 12-4

Records: OH, PH

Subjects: FC, LH

Geographical Area: Appalachia
Dates: 1866 to 1950
Size: 1-10 linear feet

---

153 **Capon Bridge Public Library**
Route 50
Capon Bridge, WV 26711

304-856-3777   Type: PL
Patricia Lee, Librarian
Mon. 11-5; Tues. 2:30-9; Wed.-Fri. 11-5

Records: MS

Subjects: CW, FC, GE, LH, MH, PW, RC, WO

Geographical Area: Appalachia
Dates: 1866 to date
Size: 1-10 linear feet

---

154 **Clarksburg-Harrison Public Library**
404 West Pike St.
Clarksburg, WV 26301

304-624-6512   Type: PL
Lloyd Leggett, Curator
Mon. 1-8; Tues.-Thurs. 9-5; Fri. 9-3;
  Sat. 9-1

Records: MS, OH, GE, PH, IA

Subjects: AG, AR, BL, BI, CW, CR, ED, EI, FC, GE, IN, LA, LI, LH, MI, MU, NR, PW, PS, PN, RT, RC, TT, WO

Geographical Area: Appalachia
Dates: Pre-1800 to date
Size: 51-150 linear feet

---

155 **Concord College Library**
Concord College
Athens, WV 24712

304-384-3115   Type: CU
Michael B. Pate
Mon.-Thurs. 8-10; Fri. 8-4; Sat. 12-4;
  Sun. 4-10

Records: MS, OH, AV, PH, IA

Subjects: ED

Geographical Area: Appalachia
Dates: 1866 to date
Size: 11-50 linear feet

156 **Gilmer County Historical Society**
Court House Annex
Glenville, WV 26351

304-462-8634   Type: HS
G. Bayard Young, President
By Appointment Only

Records: MS, PH

Subjects: AR, BI, CW, ED, GE, LI, LH, MH

Geographical Area: Appalachia
Dates: Pre-1800 to date
Size: 11-50 linear feet

157 **Gilmer Public Library**
214 Walnut St.
Glenville, WV 26351

304-462-5620   Type: PL
Kyle Emerson, Director
Mon.-Sat. 9-5

Records: OH, GE

Subjects: FC, GE, LH

Geographical Area: Appalachia
Dates: Pre-1800 to date
Size: 1-10 linear feet

158 **Greenbrier Historical Society Archives**
Greenbrier County Historical Society
100 Church St.
Lewisburg, WV 24901

304-647-5401   Type: HS
Frances A. Swope
Thurs. 1-4:30; Apr.-Nov.

Records: GE, PH

Subjects: CW, GE, LI, LH

Geographical Area: Appalachia
Dates: Pre-1800 to 1860; 1866 to 1900
Size: 1-10 linear feet

159 **Greenbrier, The CSX Hotels, Inc.**
White Sulphur Spring, WV 24986

304-536-1110   Type: BU
Robert S. Conte, Historian
By Appointment Only

Records: MS, PH

Subjects: BI, CR, RT, TT

Geographical Area: Appalachia, United States
Dates: 1801 to date
Size: 151-300 linear feet

160 **Hampshire County Public Library**
153 West Main St.
Romney, WV 26757

304-822-3185   Type: PL
Helen Scott, Librarian
Mon.-Sat. 10-5

Records: OH, GE, PH

Subjects: AG, AR, BL, BI, CW, ED, EI, FC, GE, LI, LH, MH, PW, PS, RC

Geographical Area: Appalachia
Dates: Pre-1800 to date
Size: 51-150 linear feet

161 **Hardy County Public Library**
102 North Main St.
Moorefield, WV 26836

304-538-6560   Type: PL
Marjorie Zirk, Librarian
Mon.-Sat. 9-4:30

Records: MS, GE, PH, IA

Subjects: CW, EI, GE, IN, LI, LH, RT

Geographical Area: Appalachia
Dates: Pre-1800 to date
Size:

162 **Harpers Ferry Center Library**
National Park Service History College
Harpers Ferry, WV 25425

304-535-6371   Type: OT
David Nathanson
Mon.-Thurs. 8-5; Fri. 8-4:30

Records: MS, OH, AV, PH, IA

Subjects: AR, CW, LH, MH, NR, RT

Geographical Area: Appalachia,
    United States
Dates: 1861 to date
Size: Over 1000 linear feet

163 **Harrison County
Historical Society**
123 West Main St.
Box 2074
Clarksburg, WV 26301

304-842-3073   Type: HS
Madge McDaniel, Treasurer
Mar.-Dec.: Mon. & Fri. 2-4

Records: MS, GE, PH

Subjects: AG, AR, BL, BI, CW, CR,
    ED, EI, FC, GE, IN, LA, LI, LH,
    MC, MH, MI, MU, NR, PW, PS, PN,
    RC, TT, WO

Geographical Area: Appalachia
Dates: Pre-1800 to date
Size: 151-300 linear feet

164 **Jackson County
Historical Society**
P. O. Box 22
Ripley Municipal Building, 3rd floor
Ripley, WV 25271

304-372-2831   Type: HS
Ed Rauh
By Appointment Only

Records: MS, GE, PH, IA

Subjects: AG, CW, FC, GE, LH, PW

Geographical Area: Appalachia
Dates: 1866 to 1950
Size: 11-50 linear feet

165 **James E. Morrow Library**
Marshall University
3rd Ave. and Hal Greer Blvd.
Huntington, WV 25701

304-696-2320   Type: CU
Lisle G. Brown, Curator
Mon.-Thurs. 8-10; Sat. 9-5;
    Sun. 1:30-9:30

Records: MS, OH, GE, AV, PH, IA

Subjects: AR, BL, CW, FC, GE, HS,
    LA, LH, MH, MI, MU, PN, WO

Geographical Area: Appalachia
Dates: Pre-1800 to date
Size: Over 1000 linear feet

166 **Kanawha Valley
Genealogical Society**
Myers Ave.
Dunbar, WV 25064

                                Type: OT
Carolyn M. Conner, President
Wed. 1-4

Records: MS, GE

Subjects: BL, CW, GE, IN, LH, MH

Geographical Area: Appalachia
Dates: Pre-1800 to date
Size: 51-150 linear feet

167 **Mary F. Shipper Library/LRC**   Records: MS, GE, IA
Potomac State College of
West Virginia University   Subjects: FC, GE, LH
Keyser, WV 26726

304-788-3011   Type CU   Geographical Area: Appalachia
P. S. Williams   Dates: Pre-1800 to 1860
Mon.-Thurs. 8-10; Fri. 8-5   Size: 1-10 linear feet

168 **McDowell Public Library**   Records: PH
90 Howard St.
Welch, WV 24801   Subjects: PS

304-436-3070   Type: PL   Geographical Area: Appalachia
William A. Muller, III   Dates: 1951 to date
Mon. 11-7; Tues.-Sat. 9-5   Size: 1-10 linear feet

169 **Morgan County Historical**   Records: MS, GE, PH, IA
     and Genealogical Society
Box 52   Subjects: FC, GE, LH, MU, RT
Berkeley Springs, WV 25411

304-258-2174   Type: PL   Geographical Area: Appalachia
Katheryn Allemong   Dates: Pre-1800 to date
Mon., Tues., Thurs., Fri. 10-5;   Size: 151-300 linear feet
   Wed., Sat. 9:30-1

170 **Morgantown Public Library**   Records: MS, PH, IA
West Virginia Collection
373 Spruce St.   Subjects: FC, GE, RC
Morgantown, WV 26505

304-291-7425   Type: PL   Geographical Area: Appalachia
Susan E. Swanson   Dates: 1901 to date
Mon. 9-8; Tues.-Thurs. 9-6; Fri.-Sat. 9-5   Size: 151-300 linear feet

171 **Oglebay Institute—**   Records: MS, AV, PH, IA
     Mansion Museum
Oglebay Park   Subjects: BI, LH, ST
Wheeling, WV 26003

304-242-7272   Type: MU   Geographical Area: Appalachia
T. Patrick Brennan, Curator   Dates: 1845 to date
Mon.-Sat. 9:30-5; Sun. 1-5   Size:

172 **Ohio County Public Library**   Records: MS, PH
52 16th St.
Wheeling, WV 26003   Subjects: LH

304-232-0244   Type: PL   Geographical Area: Appalachia
Bruce Farrar, Librarian   Dates:
Mon.-Thurs. 9-9; Fri. 10-5; Sat. 9-5   Size:

173 **Pendleton County**
Historical Society
Main St.
Franklin, WV 26807

304-358-7366 Type: HS
Mrs. John Harman, President
Mon.-Fri. 9-5

Records: MS, GE

Subjects: CW, GE

Geographical Area: Appalachia
Dates: Pre-1800 to date
Size:

174 **Pleasants County**
Historical Society
913 4th St.
St. Marys, WV 26170

Type: HS
Isabel Strickling, Treasurer
By Appointment Only

Records: MS, AV, PH

Subjects: FC, LH, MI

Geographical Area: Appalachia
Dates: 1901 to 1950
Size: 11-50 linear feet

175 **Pocahontas County**
Historical Society
810 2nd Ave.
Marlington, WV 24954

304-799-4973 Type: MU
William P. McNeel, Historian
Summer: Mon.-Sat. 11-5; Sun. 1-5

Records: MS, OH, PH

Subjects: FC, GE, LH, PS, RC

Geographical Area: Appalachia
Dates: 1866 to date
Size: 11-50 linear feet

176 **Potomac State College Library**
Potomac State College
Keyser, WV 26726

304-788-3011 Type: CU
Ms. Betty Howard, Librarian
Mon.-Thurs. 8-10; Fri. 8-5; Sun. 5-10

Records: MS

Subjects: BL, GE, LH

Geographical Area: Appalachia
Dates:
Size: 1-10 linear feet

177 **Pricketts Fort**
Memorial Foundation
Pricketts Fort State Park
Rt. 3
Fairmont, WV 26554

304-363-3030 Type: HS
David Elkinton
Mon.-Fri. 9-4

Records: MS, OH, GE, PH

Subjects: CR, FC, GE, LH, PW, RT

Geographical Area: Appalachia
Dates: Pre-1800 to date
Size: 11-50 linear feet

178 **Princeton Public Library**
205 Center St.
Princeton, WV 24740

304-425-3324 Type: PL
Joni L. Dempsey, Director
Mon., Tues., Thurs. 10-8;
   Wed., Fri. 10-5; Sat. 9-1

Records: MS, GE, PH

Subjects: AG, AR, BI, CR, ED, FC,
   GE, LH, MI, NR

Geographical Area: Appalachia
Dates: 1866 to date
Size: 1-10 linear feet

179 **Rainelle Public Library**
312 7th St.
Rainelle, WV 25962

304-438-5335   Type: PL
Danny McMillion, Librarian

Records: GE

Subjects: FC, LH

Geographical Area: Appalachia
Dates: Pre-1800 to 1860; 1901 to 1950
Size: 1-10 linear feet

---

180 **Raleigh County**
Public Library
221 North Kanawha St.
Beckley, WV 25801

304-255-0511   Type: PL
Susan Vidovich, Director
Mon. 9-9; Tues.-Thurs. 9-8; Fri.-Sat. 9-5

Records: MS, GE, AV, PH

Subjects: FC, LH

Geographical Area: Appalachia
Dates:
Size:

---

181 **Summers County**
Public Library
201 Temple St.
P. O. Box 9
Hinton, WV 25951

304-466-4490   Type: PL
Opal Harvey
Mon., Wed., Fri. 9-5; Tues., Thurs. 9-9;
   Sat. 9-3

Records: MS, GE, PH, IA

Subjects: AG, AR, BL, BI, CW, CR,
   ED, EI, FC, GE, HS, IN, LA, LI, LH,
   MC, MH, MI, MU, NR, PA, PW, PS,
   PN, RT, RC, SA, ST, TT, WO

Geographical Area: Appalachia,
   United States, Foreign
Dates: Pre-1800 to date
Size: 300-999 linear feet

---

182 **Tucker County**
Historical Society
Hambleton Historical Pres. Society
Box 17
Hambleton, WV 26269

304-478-2354   Type: HS
Maxine Goff Morgan
By Appointment Only

Records: MS, OH, GE, PH, IA

Subjects: CW, FC, GE, LH, MH,
   PW, RC

Geographical Area: Appalachia
Dates: Pre-1800 to date
Size: 300-999 linear feet

---

183 **Vining Library**
West Virginia Institute of Technology
Montgomery, WV 25136

304-442-3230   Type: CU
Edith Tabit
Mon.-Fri. 8-4:30; Additional Hours

Records: OH, IA

Subjects: LH

Geographical Area: Appalachia
Dates: 1866 to date
Size: 11-50 linear feet

184 **Williamson Campus Library**
Southern W. V. Community College
Armory Dr.
Williamson, WV 25661

304-235-2800   Type: CU
Carol Carlton, Librarian
Mon.-Thurs. 8:30-9 pm; Fri. 8:30-5 pm

Records: MS, OH, GE, AV, IA

Subjects: ED, FC, GE, LH, MI, MU

Geographical Area: Appalachia
Dates: Pre-1801 to date
Size: 11-50 linear feet

---

185 **WV and Regional History College**
West Virginia University
Colson Hall
Morgantown, WV 26506

304-293-3536   Type: CU
George Parkingson, Curator
Mon.-Fri. 8-5; Sat. 9-5

Records: MS, OH, GE, AV, PH, IA

Subjects: AG, AR, BL, BI, CW, CR,
    ED, EI, FC, GE, HS, IN, LA, LI, LH,
    MC, MH, MI, MU, NR, PA, PW, PS,
    PN, RT, RC, SA, ST, TT, WO

Geographical Area: Appalachia
Dates: Pre-1800 to date
Size: Over 1000 linear feet

---

186 **Yesterday's Place**
1277 South Broad St.
Summersville, WV 26651

304-872-6456   Type: MU
Harry Lynch
Sat.-Sun. 10-5

Records: MS, OH, PH

Subjects: AG, BI, CW, CR, IN, LH,
    MU, NR, WO

Geographical Area: Appalachia
Dates: Pre-1800 to date
Size:

COMING ATTRACTIONS
Kentucky

Agriculture Library
University of Kentucky   A. P. Powell
Agricultural Science Cntr-N
Lexington, KY 40546   606-257-8360

Calvary Cemetery
Diocese of Covington   M. M. Sullivan, Secretary
874 West Main St.
Lexington, KY 40505   606-252-5415

Hazard Community College Library
University of Kentucky   Eileen Haddix
Hazard, KY 41701   606-436-5721

Keeneland Association Library
U. S. Highway 60   Doris Jean Waren, Librarian
P. O. Box 1690
Lexington, KY 40592   606-254-3412

Lee County Public Library
Box V   Anna Lee Abner
Beattyville, KY 41311   606-464-8014

Lexington Cemetery Co., Inc.   Robert F. Wachs, Manager
833 West Main St.
Lexington, KY 40508   606-255-5522

**Lexington Herald-Leader County
   Library**   Lu-Ann Dunn Farrar
Main & Midland
Lexington, KY 40507   606-231-3334

Lilley Cornett Woods
Eastern Kentucky University   Michael Brotzge, Superintendant
HC 63, Box 2710
Skyline, KY 41851   606-633-5828

Living Arts and Science Center
362 Walnut St.   Susan B. Thompson, Director
Lexington, KY 40508   606-252-5222

**Prestonsburg Community
College-Library**
University of Kentucky   Sandra Robertson, Librarian
Bert Combs Dr., Johnson Building
Prestonsburg, Ky 41653   606-886-3863

Wolfe County Public Library
Main St., Box 10
Campton, KY 41301

Billye H. Adams, Librarian
606-668-6571

North Carolina

Dobson Community Library
Northwestern Regional Library
P. O. Box 237
Dobson, NC 27017

Rausie Hobson, Consultant

919-386-8208

Historic Flat Rock, Inc.
P. O. Box 295
Flat Rock, NC 28731

Edward McCandless, Secretary

Lewisville Branch Library
Forsyth Co. Public Library
Lewisville Plaza Shopping Ctr.
Lewisville, NC 27023

Laura Robbins, Supervisor

919-945-3786

Maggie Valley Public Library
Haywood County Public Library
Highway 19
Maggie, NC 28751

Kim J. Garmon, Librarian

704-926-0461

Maiden Branch Library
Catawba Co. Library
Main St.
Maiden, NC 28650

Shirley D. Sipe, Assistant

704-428-2712

Mooneyham Public Library
417 East Main St.
Forest City, NC 28043

Mary S. Costner, Librarian
704-245-2281

Museum of N. C. Handicrafts
P. O. Box 778
Waynesville, NC 28786

Mary Comwell, Director
704-452-1551

National Climatic Data Center
NOAA, Department of Commerce
Federal Building
Asheville, NC 28801

Thomas A. Prizio, Chief

704-259-0785

Old Wilkes Jail Museum
Old Wilkes, Inc.
203 North Bridge St.
Wilkesboro, NC 28697

Joan S. Baity, Curator

919-667-3712

Smith-McDowell House
283 Victoria Rd.   Julie Risher, Director
Asheville, NC 28801   704-253-9231

Spindale Public Library
101 Tanner St.   Maxine A. Harrill, Librarian
Spindale, NC 28160   704-286-3879

Traphill Branch Public Library
Wilkes County Public Library   Emma Billings
N. Wilkesboro, NC 28659   919-838-2818

South Carolina

Anderson County Historical Society
Box 785   Beth Ann Klosky, Pres.
Anderson, SC 29622   803-296-1283

Cherokee Histolrical &
  Preservation Society Museum   James Taylor, President
P. O. Box 278
Gaffney, SC 29342

Pendleton Foundation For
  Black History and Culture   Annie Webb Morse
P. O. Box 122
Pendleton, SC 29670   803-646-3792

Tennessee

Jonesborough-Washington County
  Library   Suzanne S. Tuggle, Director
Main St., Chester Inn
Jonesborough, TN 37659   615-753-4841

West Virginia

Ceredo-Kenova Public Library
Cabell County Public Library   Brenda G. Francis, Clerk
12th and Poplar Sts.
Kenova, WV 25530   304-453-2462

Cowen Public Library
P. O. Box 187, School St.   Diane Forbes, Librarian
Cowen, WV 26206   304-226-5332

Elkins-Randolph Co. Library
416 Davis Ave.
Elkins, WV 26241

Jane T. Fair, Librarian
304-636-1121

Milton Branch Library
Cabell County Public Library
1140 Smith St.
Milton, WV 25541

Elizabeth Reese, Librarian

304-743-6711

Robert F. Kidd Library
Glenville State College
Glenville, WV 26351

John Hymes, Jr., Professor
304-462-7361

Sutton Public Library
West Virginia Library Commission
General Delivery
Sutton, WV 26601

Wilma Myers, Librarian

304-765-7224

LIST OF REPOSITORIES

Georgia

Chattahoochee National Forest
U.S. Forest Service
Blairsville

Chattahoochee-Oconee N. Forest
U.S. Forest Service
Gainesville

Crown Garden and Archives
Whitfield-Murray Historical Society
Dalton

Forsyth County Heritage Foundation
P. O. Box 762
Cumming

Fox Fire Fund, Inc.
Rabun Gap

Gwinnett Historical Society
Lawrenceville

Marble Valley Historical Society
GA Room of Pickens County Library
Jasper

Mountain Regional Library
P. O. Box 157
Young Harris

N. E. Georgia Regional Library
Clarkesville

Quinlan Art Center
Gainesville Art Association
Gainesville

Sequoyah Regional Library
Canton

Southeastern Railway & Museum
National Railway Historical Society
Duluth

Vann House Historic Site
GA Department of National Resources
Chatsworth

Kentucky

Appalachian Museum
Berea College
Berea

Appalshop Films, Inc.
Whitesburg

Ashland Public Library
Ashland

Cumberland Gap National Histical Park
Middlesboro

Eastern Kentucky University Archives
Eastern Kentucky University
Richmond

Greenup County Public Library
Greenup

Harlan County Genealogical
Society
Harlan

Harlan County Public Library
Harlan

Henderson Settlement Mission
United Methodist Church Project
Frakes

Hunt-Morgan House
Blue Grass Trust for Historical Pres.
Lexington

Jenkins Public Library
Jenkins

Johnson County Public Library
Paintsville

Kentucky Depart. of Mines and Minerals
Lexington

Laurel County Library
London

Lexington Public Library
Lexington

Middlesboro-Bell County Public Library
Middlesboro

O'Rear Robinson Library
Pikeville College Media Center
Pikeville

Owsley County Historical Society
Kentucky Department for Libraries
Booneville

Perry County Genealogical and
Historical Society
Hazard

Pike County Historical Society
Pikeville

Pine Mountain Settlement School
E. J. Carr
Pine Mountain

Pineville-Bell County Public
Library
Pineville

Rockcastle County Public Library
Mount Vernon

Special Collections
Berea College
Berea

Special Collections & Archives
University of Kentucky
Lexington

Transylvania University Library
Transylvania University
Lexington

United Methodist Church
Archives and History
Lexington

North Carolina

Alleghany Historical—
Genealogical Society, Inc.
Sparta

Appalachia Room Special
Collections
Mars Hill

Ashe County Public Library
Appalachian Regional Library
West Jefferson

Asheville-Buncombe Library System
Pack Memorial & Admin. Office
Asheville

Blue Ridge Parkway National Park Service Asheville	Broad River Genealogical Society Shelby
Burke County Public Library Morganton	Caldwell County Public Library Lenoir
Canton Public Library Branch of Haywood County Library Canton	Carl Sandburg National Historical Site National Park Service Flat Rock
Catawba County Historical Museum Catawba County Historical Association Newton	Cherokee County Historical Museum Murphy
Coweeta Hydrologic Laboratory Southeastern Forest Exp. Sta. Otto	Cradle of Forestry in America U.S. Forest Service Pisgah Forest
D. D. Dougherty Library Appalachian State University Boone	Davie County Public Library Mocksville
Dry Ridge Historical Museum North Buncombe Library Weaverville	Eastern Cabarrus Historical Society Mount Pleasant
Elbert Ivey Memorial Public Library Hickory	Historical Foundation of the Presbyterian & Reformed Church Montreat
Historic Resources Commission of Asheville & Buncombe County Asheville	Hunter Library Western Carolina University Cullowhee
Jacob S. Mauney Memorial Library Kings Mountain	James Larkin Pearson Library Wilkes Community College Wilkesboro
Macon County Public Library Fontana Regional Library Franklin	Mayland Technical College Spruce Pine
Moravian Archives Moravian Church in America Winston-Salem	Moravian Music Foundation Winston-Salem

Museum of the Cherokee Indian
Drama Road
Cherokee

Museum of Waldensian History
Waldensian Presbyterian Church
Valdese

N. C. Baptist Historical Collection
Wake Forest University
Winston-Salem

National Forests in NC
U.S. Forest Service
Asheville

Old Bumcombe County Genealogical
Society, Inc.
Asheville

Polk County Historical
Association's Museum
Tryon

Thomas Wolfe Memorial
NC Department of Cultural Resources
Asheville

Transylvania County Library
Brevard

University Archives
Wake Forest University
Winston-Salem

W. L. Eury Appalachian Collection
Appalachian State University
Boone

Yadkin Historical Society
Yadkin County Library
Yadkinville

Zebulon B. Vance Birthplace
NC Department of Archives & History
Weaverville

South Carolina

Greenville County Historical Society
Greenville County Library
Greenville

Oconee County Library
Walhalla

Pendleton Dist. Hist. & Rec. Comm.
Pendleton

Pickens County Historical Society
Pickens

Pickens County Library
Easley

Special Collections
Robert Muldrow Cooper Library
Clemson

Special Collections/Archives
Furman University Library
Greenville

Tennessee

Andrew Johnson National Historical Site
U.S. National Park Service
Greeneville

Archives and Special Cols.
Carson-Newman College Library
Jefferson City

Archives of Appalachia East Tennessee State University Johnson City	Bradley County Historical Society Cleveland
Calvin M. McClung Collection Knox County Public Library Knoxville	Carroll Reece Museum East Tennessee State University Johnson City
Children's Museum of Oak Ridge 461 West Outer Dr. Oak Ridge	Cleveland State Community College Library Cleveland
Dayton Library Dayton	Dulin Gallery of Art Knoxville
E. W. King Library King College, Inc. Bristol	Elizabethton Public Library Elizabethton
Fort Sanders Regional Medical Center-Nursing Library Knoxville	Frank H. McClung Museum University of Tennessee Knoxville
Great Smoky Mountains National Park Gatlinburg	H. B. Stamps Memorial Library Rogersville
Hardwick Johnston Memorial Library Hiwassee College Madisonville	Kingsport Public Library Kingsport
Merner-Pfeiffer Library Tennessee Wesleyan College Athens	Morristown Hamblen Library Morristown
Norris Dam State Park Will G. & Helen H. Lenoir Museum Norris	Oak Ridge Public Library Civic Center Oak Ridge
P. H. Welshimer Memorial Library Milligan College Milligan College	Parrott-Wood Library Branch of Jefferson County Library Strawberry Plains
Penecostal Research Center Penecostal Resource Center Cleveland	Quillen-Dishner College of Medicine Library Johnson City
Restoration Movement Archives Emmanuel School of Religion Johnson City	Rose Center Museum 442 West 2nd North St. Morristown

Special Collections Library University of Tennessee Knoxville	Speedwell Manor Speedwell Heritage Foundation Knoxville
Sullivan County Public Library Box 157 Blountville	Sycamore Shoals State Historical Area Elizabethton
Tennessee Valley Authority Chattanooga	Tusculum College Library Tusculum College Greenville
Unicoi County Historical Society Unicoi County Library Erwin	Veterans Adminstration Medical Center Mountain Home

Virginia

Blue Ridge Heritage Archive Ferrum College Ferrum	Buchanan County Public Library Grundy
Carol M. Newman Library Virginia Polytechnic Institute Blacksburg	Easley Library Bluefield College Bluefield
Fishburn Library Hollins College Roanoke	Grayson County Historical Society Independence
Historical Society of Washington County, Virginia, Inc. Abingdon	Historical Crab Orchard Museum Tazewell
Holston Conference Archives Kelly Library Emory	John Cook Wyllie Library Clinch Valley College of the Wise
John Preston McConnell Library Radford University Radford	Kelly Library Emory & Henry College Emory
Montgomery-Floyd Reg. Library Christianburg	Patrick County Branch Blue Ridge Regional Library Stuart
Pearisburg Public Library Pearisburg	Pulaski County Library Pulaski

Roanoke College Library
Roanoke College
Salem

Smithfield Plantation House
Montgomery Branch of APVA
Blackburg

Smyth County Museum and
Society, Inc.
Marion

Tazewell County Public Library
Tazewell

Wilderness Road Regional Museum
New River Historical Society
Newbern

West Virginia

Alexander Campbell Archives
T. W. Phillips Library
Bethany

Brooke County Historical Society
Brooke County Public Library
Wellsburg

Burnsville Public Library
Upshur County Library
Burnsville

Capon Bridge Public Library
Capon Bridge

Clarksburg-Harrison Public Library
Clarksburg

Concord College Library
Concord College
Athens

Gilmer County Historical Society
Glenville

Gilmer Public Library
Glenville

Greenbrier Historical Society Archives
Greenbrier County Historical Society
Lewisburg

Greenbrier, The
CSX Hotels, Inc.
White Sulphur Spring

Hampshire County Public Library
Romney

Hardy County Public Library
Moorefield

Harpers Ferry Center Library
National Park Service History Col.
Harpers Ferry

Harrison County Historical Society
123 West Main St.
Clarksburg

Jackson County Historical Society
P. O. Box 22
Ripley

James E. Morrow Library
Marshall University
Huntington

Kanawha Valley Genealogical Society
Dunbar

Mary F. Shipper Library/LRC
Potomac State College of
West Virginia University
Keyser

McDowell Public Library Welch	Morgan County Historical and Genealogical Society Berkeley Springs
Morgantown Public Library West Virginia Collection Morgantown	Olegbay Institute— Mansion Museum Wheeling
Ohio County Public Library Wheeling	Pendleton County Historical Society Franklin
Pleasants County Historical Society St. Marys	Pocahontas County Historical Society Marlinton
Potomac State College Library Potomac State College Keyser	Pricketts Fort Memorial Foundation Pricketts Fort State Park Fairmont
Princetown Public Library Princeton	Rainelle Public Library Rainelle
Raleigh County Public Library Beckley	Summers County Public Library 201 Temple St. Hinton
Tucker County Historical Society Hambleton Historical Pres. Society Hambleton	Vining Library West Virginia Institute of Montgomery
Williamson Campus Library Southern W. V. Community College Williamson	WV and Regional History College West Virginia University Morgantown
Yesterday's Place Summersville	

RECORD TYPE INDEX

The following is a list of record types with the corresponding reference numbers of the repositories which have those kinds of records.

AUDIO-VISUAL—GA: 2, 5, **KY:** 14, 15, 17, 18, 20, 22, 23, 27, 38, 39, 41, **NC:** 43, 50, 52, 55, 61, 63, 65, 69, 72, 73, 75, 76, 78, 79, 81, **SC:** 82, 87, 88, 89, 91, 93, 94, 95, 97, 113, 116, 117, 118, 125, **VA:** 129, 131, 133, 139, 140, 142, 147, 149, **W. VA:** 151, 155, 162, 165, 171, 174, 180, 184, 185

GENEALOGICAL CHARTS—GA: 3, 6, 7, 9, 13, **KY:** 19, 20, 21, 23, 25, 27, 30, 31, 32, 33, 34, 36, 37, 38, 39, **NC:** 42, 43, 44, 47, 48, 49, 52, 58, 60, 61, 63, 64, 67, 69, 71, 72, 74, 76, 77, 79, 80, 81, **SC:** 83, 84, 87, 88, **TN:** 89, 91, 92, 93, 94, 99, 100, 103, 104, 108, 123, 127, **VA:** 130, 131, 133, 134, 135, 136, 137, 138, 139, 142, 143, 144, 148, 149, **W. VA:** 150, 151, 154, 157, 158, 160, 161, 163, 164, 165, 166, 167, 169, 173, 177, 178, 179, 180, 181, 182, 184, 185

ORAL HISTORIES—GA: 2, 3, 5, 11, 13, **KY:** 14, 17, 18, 19, 20, 21, 22, 23, 25, 27, 30, 34, 35, 36, 37, 38, 39, 41, **NC:** 42, 43, 44, 46, 48, 50, 51, 53, 55, 57, 61, 65, 67, 71, 72, 73, 76, 78, 79, **SC:** 84, 86, 88, **TN:** 89, 91, 92, 93, 95, 99, 103, 108, 113, 116, 117, 118, 124, 125, 127, 128, **VA:** 129, 131, 133, 134, 136, 137, 138, 139, 140, 142, 143, 149, **W. VA:** 151, 152, 154, 155, 157, 160, 162, 165, 175, 177, 182, 183, 184, 185, 186

PHOTOGRAPHS—GA: 1, 2, 3, 4, 5, 6, 7, 11, 12, 13, **KY:** 14, 15, 16, 17, 18, 19, 20, 21, 22, 23, 24 25, 27, 28, 30, 31, 34, 35, 36, 38, 39, 40, **NC:** 43, 44, 45, 46, 47, 50, 51, 52, 53, 54, 55, 58, 59, 60, 61, 63, 65, 69, 70, 71, 72, 73, 75, 76, 77, 78, 79, **SC:** 82, 83, 84, 85, 86, 87, 88, 89, **TN:** 90, 91, 92, 93, 94, 95, 98, 99, 101, 102, 103, 106, 113, 114, 115, 116, 117, 118, 119, 121, 122, 124, 125, 126, 127, 128, **VA:** 129, 130, 131, 133, 134, 135, 136, 137, 138, 139, 140, 141, 142, 146, 147, 148, 149, **W. VA:** 150, 151, 152, 154, 155, 156, 158, 159, 160, 161, 162, 163, 164, 165, 168, 169, 170, 171, 172, 174, 175, 177, 178, 180, 181, 182, 185, 186

SUBJECT INDEX

The following is a list of subjects with the corresponding reference numbers of the repositories which have manuscripts related to each subject.

AGRICULTURE—GA: 1, 2, 5, 8, 13, **KY**: 14, 17, 23, 38, 39, 40, **NC**: 43, 44, 46, 51, 52, 53, 57, 58, 67, 72, 73, 75, 77, 79, 80, **SC**: 84, 85, 87, **TN**: 91, 93, 95, 99, 102, 119, 124, 125, 128, **VA**: 129, 131, 134, 136, 139, 140, 142, 143, 146, 147, 149, **W.VA**: 154, 160, 163, 164, 178, 181, 185, 186

ART/ARCHITECTURE—GA: 5, 10, 13, **KY**: 14, 17, 23, 34, 38, 39, 44, 45, 48, 51, 52, 58, 62, 69, 72, 75, 77, 79, **SC**: 82, **TN**: 91, 93, 94, 95, 98, 99, 102, 124, 125, 128, **VA**: 129, 133, 134, 135, 142, 146, **W.VA**: 154, 156, 160, 162, 163, 165, 178, 181, 185

BLACKS—GA: 5, 13, **KY**: 17, 18, 23, 38, 39, 41, **NC**: 43, 44, 48, 52, 53, 57, 58, 61, 63, 72, 74, 75, 77, 79, **SC**: 84, 87, **TN**: 91, 92, 93, 95, 99, 112, 125, 128, **VA**: 129, 133, 134, 136, 137, 139, 142, 143, **W.VA**: 154, 160, 163, 165, 166, 176, 181, 185

BUSINESS/INDUSTRY—GA: 2, 5, 7, 11, 12, 13, **KY**: 16, 17, 18, 23, 24, 30, 34, 38, 39, 40, **NC**: 43, 44, 48, 51, 52, 57, 58, 63, 67, 70, 72, 73, 77, 79, **SC**: 82, 84, 87, **TN**: 91, 92, 93, 94, 95, 112, 115, 119, 121, 122, 124, 125, **VA**: 129, 131, 134, 135, 136, 138, 139, 140, 142, 143, 147, 149, **W.VA**: 151, 154, 156, 159, 160, 163, 171, 178, 181, 185, 186

CIVIL WAR—GA: 2, 3, 5, 7, 11, 12, **KY**: 17, 18, 19, 20, 23, 25, 34, 38, 39, **NC**: 43, 44, 45, 48, 49, 51, 52, 57, 58, 59, 61, 63, 67, 69, 72, 74, 75, 77, 79, 80, 81, **SC**: 82, 84, 85, 88, **TN**: 89, 90, 91, 92, 93, 94, 95, 99, 102, 110, 112, 115, 121, 122, 127, **VA**: 131, 133, 134, 135, 136, 137, 138, 140, 142, 143, 144, 147, 149, **W.VA**: 151, 153, 154, 156, 158, 160, 161, 162, 163, 164, 165, 166, 173, 181, 182, 185, 186

CRAFTS—GA: 1, 2, 5, 8, 13, **KY**: 14, 17, 23, 38, 39, 43, 46, 52, 58, 67, 70, 77, 79, 81, **TN**: 91, 93, 95, 102, 124, 125, **VA**: 129, 131, 134, 136, 139, 143, 147, **W.VA**: 154, 159, 163, 177, 178, 181, 185, 186

EDUCATION—GA: 1, 5, 11, 13, **KY**: 14, 17, 18, 19, 22, 23, 25, 31, 34, 38, 39, **NC**: 43, 44, 48, 51, 52, 53, 55, 56, 57, 58, 59, 61, 63, 69, 70, 72, 73, 77, 79, 80, **SC**: 82, 85, 87, 88, **TN**: 90, 91, 92, 93, 95, 99, 101, 112, 114, 115, 116, 119, 121, 123, 124, 125, 126, 127, **VA**: 129, 131, 132, 133, 134, 135, 136, 137, 138, 139, 140, 142, 143, 147, 149, **W.VA**: 150, 151, 154, 155, 156, 160 163, 178, 181, 184, 185

EHTNIC GROUPS/IMMIGRATION—GA: 5, 13, **KY**: 39, **NC**: 44, 51, 52, 67, 70, 71, 74, 77, 79, **TN**: 93, 95, 111, 124, **VA**: 129, 134, 137, 139, 143, 146, **W.VA**: 154, 160, 161, 163, 181, 185

FAMILY/COMMUNITY LIFE—GA: 1, 2, 3, 5, 6, 7, 8, 13, **KY**: 14, 16, 17, 18, 20, 21, 22, 23, 25, 31, 34, 38, 39, **NC**: 43, 44, 48, 49, 50, 52, 53, 58, 59, 61, 63, 67, 69, 70, 72, 75, 76, 77, 78, 79, 80, **SC**: 82, 83, 84, 85, 86, 88, **TN**: 90, 91, 92, 93, 94, 95, 96, 99, 101, 102, 116, 119, 122, 124, 125, 127, 128, **VA**: 129, 131, 133, 134, 135, 136, 137, 138, 139, 140, 142, 143, 144, 146, 148, 149, **W.VA**: 152, 153, 154, 157, 160, 163, 164, 165, 167, 169, 170, 174, 175, 177, 178, 179, 180, 181, 182, 184, 185

GENEALOGY—GA: 3, 4, 5, 6, 7, 9, 11, 13, **KY**: 17, 18, 19, 20, 21, 23, 25, 30, 31, 32, 33, 34, 36, 37, 38, 39, **NC**: 42, 43, 44, 47, 48, 49, 52, 57, 58, 59, 60, 61, 63, 64, 66, 67, 69, 71, 72, 74, 75, 76, 77, 79, 80, 81, **SC**: 82, 83, 84, 86, 87, 88, **TN**: 89, 90, 91, 92, 93, 94, 95, 97, 99, 100, 103, 104, 108, 111, 112, 123, 124, 127, **VA**: 130, 131, 133, 134, 135, 136, 137, 138, 139, 142, 143, 144, 146, 147, 148, 149, **W.VA**: 150, 151, 153, 154, 156, 157, 158, 160, 161, 163, 164, 165, 166, 167, 169, 170, 173, 175, 176, 177, 178, 181, 182, 184, 185

HEALTH SCIENCES—GA: 5, **KY**: 14, 18, 23, 38, 39, 40, **NC**: 63, 77, 79, **TN**: 91, 93, 95, 101, 117, 122, 125, 128, **VA**: 143, **W.VA**: 165, 181, 185

INDIANS—GA: 1, 2, 3, 4, 5, 6, 7, 8, 11, 13, **KY**: 17, 19, **NC**: 43, 44, 48, 52, 53, 58, 59, 61, 63, 69, 70, 72, 74, 75, 77, 79, **SC**: 85, **TN**: 92, 93, 95, 102, 121, 124, 125, 127, **VA**: 134, 135, 136, 137, 143, 146, 147, **W.VA**:154, 161, 163, 166, 181, 185, 186

LABOR—GA: 5, 11, 12, **KY**: 23, 38, 39, **NC**: 44, 51, 58, 72, 77, 79, **SC**: 84, **TN**: 91, 92, 93, 95, 124, 125, **VA**: 129, 131, 134, 136, 138, 140, 142, 143, **W.VA**: 154, 163, 165, 181, 185

LITERATURE—GA: 2, 3, 8, 11, **KY**: 17, 18, 19, 23, 31, 34, 38, 39, **NC**: 43, 45, 51, 52, 58, 63, 69, 72, 75, 76, 77, 79, **SC**: 82, 87, 88, **TN**: 91, 93, 95, 99, 121, 122, **VA**: 131, 134, 135, 136, 142, 143, **W.VA**:154, 156, 158, 160, 161, 163, 181, 185

LOCAL HISTORY—GA: 2, 3, 4, 5, 6, 7, 8, 11, 13, **KY**: 17, 18, 19, 20, 21, 22, 23, 24, 25, 27, 28, 30, 31, 33, 34, 35, 36, 38, 39, 40, **NC**: 42, 43, 44, 45, 46, 48, 49, 50, 52, 53, 55, 56, 57, 58, 59, 60, 61, 63, 66, 67, 69, 70, 72, 74, 75, 76, 77, 79, 80, 81, **SC**: 82, 83, 84, 85, 86, 87, **TN**: 89, 90, 91, 92, 93, 94, 95, 96, 97, 99, 100, 101, 102, 104, 106, 108, 110, 111, 112, 113, 115, 116, 119, 121, 122, 124, 126, 127, 128, **VA**: 129, 131, 132, 133, 134, 135, 136, 137, 138, 139, 140, 141, 142, 143, 144, 146, 147, 148, 149, **W.VA**: 151, 152, 153, 154, 156, 157, 158, 160, 161, 162, 163, 164, 165, 166, 167, 169, 171, 172, 174, 175, 176, 177, 178, 179, 180, 181, 182, 183, 184, 185, 186

MASS COMMUNICATIONS—KY: 23, **NC**: 77, 79, **SC**: 91, 93, **W.VA**: 163, 181, 185

MILITARY HISTORY (except Civil War)**—GA**: 4, **KY**: 20, 23, 39, **NC**: 44, 48, 52, 59, 72, 77, 79, 80, **SC**: 87, **TN**: 93, 94, 119, 121, 124, 127, 128, **VA**: 131, 135, 136, 137, 146, **W.VA**: 153, 156, 160, 162, 163, 165, 166, 181, 182, 185

MINING—GA: 1, 2, 5, 7, 11, **KY**: 14, 15, 17, 24, 25, 26, 34, 38, 39, **NC**: 44, 48, 63, 67, 72, 75, 77, 79, **SC**: 91, 93, 94, 95, 99, 112, 115, 124, 125, 131, 135, 136, 138, 139, 140, 143, 151, 154, 163, 165, 174, 178, 181, 184, 185

MUSIC—GA: 5, 13, **KY**: 14, 17, 23, 38, 39, **NC**: 43, 44, 45, 51, 52, 58, 59, 61, 69, 70, 72, 76, 77, 79, **SC**: 88, 91, 93, 94, 95, 116, 128, 129, 134, 136, 138, 139, 142, 143, 149, 154, 163, 165, 169, 181, 184, 185, 186

NATURAL RESOURCES/CONSERVATION—GA: 1, 2, **KY**: 17, 18, 35, 38, 39, **NC**: 45, 46, 48, 54, 55, 57, 63, 73, 77, 79, **SC**: 87, **TN**: 91, 92, 93, 95, 102, 103, 125, **VA**: 134, 136, 138, 143, **W.VA**: 154, 162, 163, 178, 181, 185, 186

PERFORMING ARTS (except music)—**KY**: 17, 23, 38, 39, **NC**: 45, 63, 77, 79, **SC-TN**: 91, 93, 95, 121, **VA**: 129, 134, 135, 143, **W.VA**: 181, 185

PIONEERS/WESTWARD EXPANSION—**GA**: 1, 4, 6, 13, **KY**: 17, 23, 25, 39, 40, **NC**: 44, 48, 52, 58, 69, 77, 79, **TN**: 93, 95, 99, 103, 112, 121, 124, 127, **VA**: 131, 134, 135, 136, 137, 143, 146, **W.VA**: 153, 154, 160, 163, 164, 177, 181, 182, 185

POLITICS/GOVERNMENT—STATE AND LOCAL—**GA**: 5, 6, 8, 11, 13, **KY**: 17, 18, 23, 25, 38, 39, **NC**: 44, 48, 52, 56, 63, 70, 72, 75, 77, 78, 79, **SC**: 82, 85, 87, **TN**: 89, 91, 92, 93, 94, 95, 99, 112, 115, 119, 121, 124, 128, **VA**: 131, 134, 135, 136, 140, 142, 143, 144, 146, **W.VA**: 154, 160, 163, 168, 175, 181, 185

POLITICS/GOVERNMENT—NATIONAL—**GA**: 5, **KY**: 17, 18, 23, 38, 39, **NC**: 46, 51, 63, 72, 77, 78, **SC**: 87, **TN**: 89, 91, 93, 94, 95, 121, 124, **VA**: 131, 135, 136, 146, 154, **W.VA**: 163, 165, 181, 185

RECREATION/TOURISM—**GA**: 1, 2, 5, 13, **KY**: 17, 18, 23, 39, **NC**: 45, 63, 70, 73, 77, 79, **SC**: 84, **TN**: 93, 94, 95, 103, 124, 125, 128, **VA**: 129, 134, 135, 136, 139, 142, 143, **W.VA**: 154, 159, 161, 162, 169, 177, 181, 185

RELIGION/CHURCH HISTORY—**GA**: 3, 4, 5, 6, 7, 8, 11, 13, **KY**: 14, 17, 18, 22, 23, 31, 32, 34, 35, 38, 39, 41, 43, 44, 46, 48, 52, 53, 57, 58, 59, 61, 63, 68, 69, 72, 75, 77, 78, 79, 80, **SC**: 84, 85, 88, **TN**: 90, 91, 92, 93, 94, 95, 96, 99, 106, 110, 111, 114, 115, 116, 118, 119, 121, 123, 124, 126, 127, **VA**: 129, 131, 133, 134, 135, 136, 137, 138, 139, 140, 142, 144, 147, 149, **W.VA**: 150, 151, 153, 154, 160, 163, 170, 175, 181, 182, 185

SOCIAL ACTION—**GA**: 5, **KY**: 17, 18, 23, 38, 39, **NC**: 44, 61, 77, 79, **TN**: 91, 93, 95, 112, 125, **VA**: 138, **W.VA**: 181, 185

SCIENCE/TECHNOLOGY—**GA**: 1, 5, **KY**: 17, 18, 23, 35, 39, **NC**: 54, 72, 77, 79, **SC**: 87, **TN**: 91, 93, 94, 95, 101, 121, 125, **VA**: 131, 134, **W.VA**: 171, 181, 185

TRANSPORTATION/TRAVEL—**GA**: 2, 5, 12, 13, **KY**: 17, 19, 23, 38, 39, **NC**: 44, 52, 53, 72, 73, 77, 79, 80, **TN**: 91, 93, 95, 119, 124, 125, **VA**: 129, 131, 134, 135, 136, 139, 140, 142, 149, **W.VA**: 151, 154, 159, 163, 181, 185

WOMEN—**GA**: 5, **KY**: 14, 15, 17, 18, 23, 38, 39, **NC**: 44, 48, 52, 53, 58, 61, 63, 69, 72, 77, 79, 80, **SC**: 82, **TN**: 90, 91, 93, 94, 95, 116, 119, 124, 125, **VA**: 129, 131, 133, 134, 135, 136, 137, 139, 140, 142, 143, **W.VA**: 153, 154, 163, 165, 181, 185, 186

Made in United States
Orlando, FL
22 March 2026